EXPERIENTIAL EVENTS

An Event Designer's Almanac

Dr. DEEPAK SWAMINATHAN

Notion Press

Old No. 38, New No. 6
McNichols Road, Chetpet
Chennai - 600 031

First Published by Notion Press 2018
Copyright © Deepak Swaminathan 2018
All Rights Reserved.

ISBN 978-1-64249-075-6

BOOK REVIEW –
"THE ART OF BUILDING EXPERIENTIAL EVENTS" BY Dr. DEEPAK SWAMINATHAN

"Deepak has used his wide and rich experience of event conceptualization, planning and management to script his first book on this subject. He has broadly covered the scientific approach deployed in mapping the Experiential Quotient which provides an effective guide for producers of events. Every chapter of the book features a real-life case study to illustrate key concepts and ideas to tackle any challenges they may face in managing events. As you read the book, Deepak's extensive "On-Ground" experience is evident in every word."

– Sunil Misra, Director General, IEEMA, India

Event management has developed into a major promotional phenomenon in the world of business today and any business that wants to sustain itself cannot afford to dispense with the predominant need for event management which has grown into an integral, inseparable component of a business. Business itself is a mega event and event management fuses into it harmoniously. Today, no business worth the name can turn a blind eye to event management but at its own peril.

This book 'The Art of Building Experiential Events' is exhaustively informative covering all the vital aspects of event management. The very chapterization clearly indicates the comprehensive grasp of the subject by the author. Enormous pains have been taken to compile massive details of event management. It primarily deals with brand exposure through appealing episodes to the target audience with a singular focus on establishing the brand in such a way that revenue generation is guaranteed. Manufacturers, product or service, customers, price tag and brand image form the major factors involved in event management and as each segment encompasses varieties, it requires expertise to plan and organize the event that promotes the business. Expertise in reality excels in giving attention to all details, from small to serious, without prejudice. And to achieve this task, this book helps most effectively. No details have been left. In short, this book more or less like an encyclopedia is a must for any business that aims at sustainability. It is a book of reference and a manual of execution.

– Dr. R.Lakshmipathy, Publisher – Dinamalar

Deepak Swaminathan is a man of many talents and has worked in various media organisations, been an entrepreneur and now done his doctoral thesis in the field of "Experimental designing in Event management."

He founded Media Point a leading event management company, that is able to successfully run events across various geographies and scale.

This book 'The Art of Building Experiential Events', is a layman's guide into the complex but unorganised field of event management in India.

He digs deep into his experience in retaining a large number of clients, a puts those insights lucidly, in mapping through scientific grids the Clients expectations.

I believe he has written due to unabiding passion in helping get event management activity a recognised industry status in our country.

I wish him the very best in this endeavour.

– Rajiv Menon, Director, Cinematographer, Writer

R K SWAMY BBDO

SRINIVASAN K SWAMY

Chairman & Managing Director

Foreword

I have known Deepak for over two decades now. I first met him when he joined us in one of our group companies, HansaVision, to market commercial time on television serials. That was in March 1995. He gave us three and a half valuable years of his life, and as head of marketing, significantly contributed to the growth and prosperity of our business. But we always knew that he is made of a different mettle, the kind entrepreneurs are made of! We therefore were not surprised when he left us to start Media Point in September 1998. To be fair to him, though he left our employ, he always looked to us as an extended family and showed much kindness and courtesy, which is the hallmark of any 'service' business. It is little surprise therefore that he succeeded in the multiple service businesses he subsequently started.

Since inception of Media Point, he has demonstrated that no event is too big or complex for him. Every one of their 4000+ events (and that's a lot, over 200 events annually on an average), was executed without a hitch and much to the delight of their customers. He always had a passion for details and there can be no better fit than the Events business for him, which is all about attention to details. Every page in this book is a demonstration of that and he has proudly shared his vast and rich experience in this space. Further, Deepak's deep understanding of the Events Industry is seen in the explanations that he calls attention to, which is rooted in clients' interactions and executions of real time projects.

This is perhaps the first book to have been written exclusively with examples from India and the issues that relate to this country. In one of the several highpoints of the book, Deepak brings to our attention how the National Anthem has to be used in an event, keeping in mind the strong and diverse cultural beliefs and sensitivities of our people.

The book is a good beginner's guide, as much as a professional's guide. It elaborately defines what constitutes event management, provides details on how to manage client's expectations, the quality of human resources required in this regard and how to design different types of events. It features 16 chapters, which sequentially dovetail different well thought out topics, each giving practical hints and lessons on how to go about this business.

The infographics are unique, and were created from the author's own engagement with the industry. The checklists provided are excellent aids to developing and managing an event. The author magnanimously shares details of various kinds of designs used in various situations, which is the core to any event.

"The Art of Building Experiential Events – An Event Designer's Almanac" - is a major contribution by Deepak to a somewhat fledgling events industry, which is slowly being recognised as a valuable profession. He has strived hard to provide a useful guide that should be welcomed by all marketing professionals, practising managers, and young students who wish to pursue experiential marketing as a profession.

Srinivasan K Swamy

R K SWAMY BBDO PRIVATE LIMITED, REGD. OFFICE FILM CHAMBER BUILDING, 605 & 606 ANNA SALAI, CHENNAI 600 006
PHONE 044 2829 2299 FAX 044 2829 5557 EMAIL skswamy@rksbbdo.com
OFFICES ALSO AT BENGALURU, HYDERABAD, KOCHI, KOLKATA, MUMBAI, NEW DELHI

GOOD WE DECIDED & ENGAGED THE PROFESSIONAL EVENT AGENCY, THEY SURPASSED THE EXPECTATIONS

CONTENTS

                                                                 Contents

Respect and love your work with all your heart, and experience the manifestation of abundance that embraces you forever.

– Deepak Swaminathan

Chapter 1

EVENT MANAGEMENT – THE ACTIVITY IN TODAY'S CONTEXT

a. What is Event Management?

In the context of business of events, it is an activity that connects products/service with end users or with the channel that aids in reaching the product or service to the consumers or end users.

Event is also defined as a medium of experience that enables us to communicate the message of a product/service/experience/training/hospitality to the prospect. A conglomeration of interested/prospective users towards identifying an opportunity to associate/experience a brand/product/service is defined as an event.

Definition of Event Management

Event management is the detailed application of "planning-organizing-managing" in creation and development of events such as celebrity shows, corporate shows, festivals, conferences, ceremonies, formal parties, symposiums or conventions. It involves the study of a brand/service, identifying the target audience, creating an event concept, planning the logistics and coordinating the technical aspects before actually unveiling the event.

The process of planning and coordinating the event is usually referred to as event management, which could include resource planning, estimate and budgeting, content and context evaluation, scheduling, site selection, acquiring necessary permits, logistics planning, designing presentations, graphics and creative development, lining up designing décor, event security, catering and emergency plans.

b. History of Event Management

The early days of events were primarily associated with bringing together groups of people to deliver a message or to participate in festivals.

This may also involve gathering of people for display of information, communication of information, a social cause, towards building harmony and goodwill; ceremonial events like installing a leader; or an image building exercise for a theatre personality and religious.

Religious events that would instil devotion and to spread the message of warmth and peace.

c. The Early Events

17th Century – Events were confined to installation of Kings and for religious purposes.

18th Century – Regionalized festivals and sports were big celebrations that brought people together.

19th Century – Olympics is touted to be the first large-scale professionally managed event.

Cricket began to get popular and promotions alongside matches became the order of the day.

20th Century – Mini versions of the Olympics across the sphere of sports came up, festivals of faiths evolved; music shows were staged with entrance cards, prayer meetings for the welfare of the world were staged and brands capitalized on the conglomeration of people to promote.

21st Century – Events evolved as a fine medium of communication. Technology deployment made events move from just a promotion platform to an experience platform. Events became a part of all promotions that would help brands/service reach the prospect.

d. Evolution of Event Management as a Business

Event management evolved, from being an opportunity to get people together evolved into a formidable part of the communication platform. With the advent of technology and professionalism, event management came with a host of benefits that benefitted brands and services greatly. Event management with a feed of communication tools, offers tremendous value to the brand/service that is being promoted. Event management today helps in bringing the end user closer to the brand/service thereby increasing the visibility and interest quotients. The benefits that event management brought are

- Direct engagement with the prospect.
- First-hand feedback of the brand/service that was part of the event.

- Increased customer delight with hands-on experience.

- Increase in footfalls for brands/services.

- Greater reach to a specifically defined audience.

- Customized experiences for discerning prospects.

- Cost efficient exercise to reach prospects.

Events feature as a top priority among promotion and communication tools. With defined objectives and time-bound action plans, events have become key promotional tools. Events have become independent verticals that work in tandem with the whole communication wheel planning and delivering solutions that increase the curiosity element apart from offering "first-hand experience" for end users. Events act as a bridge between the "corporate/brand objective" to reach the "right market and prospect."

Presenting below a broad perspective of the promotional tools that are a mainstay in reaching brands/services to the prospects.

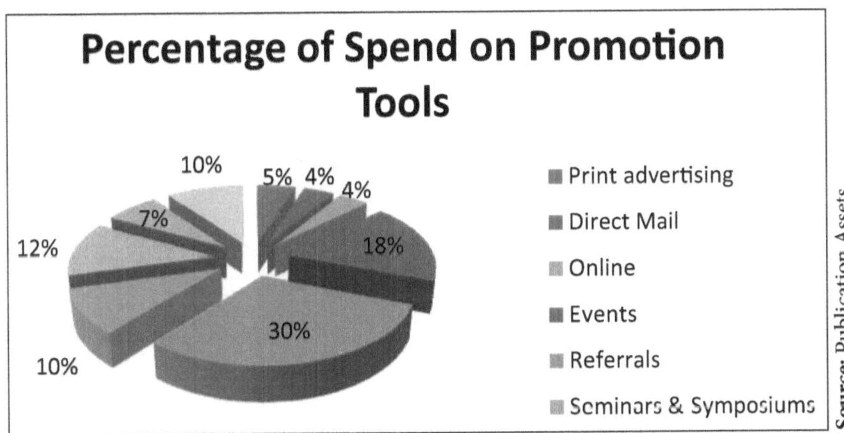

The factors that make event management a core part of promotions

- A well-designed event reflects the "power" of the brand/service.

- A well-conceived event leaves a lasting impact in the mind of the prospect.

- A well-managed event increases the "interest quotient" for a prospect.

- An opportunity to provide a holistic experience for the owner and the participant.

- High brand recall has been recorded every time a prospect gets a first-hand experience.

- The communication can be measured and delivered and that increases the opportunity.
- Lasting retention through intelligent and strategic interaction.
- Systems to measure the success quotient.

The event industry has evolved over the years and has grown considerably both in size and stature. The proliferation of TV channels and newspapers mean that advertisers have begun to opt for experiential marketing (event management) instead. According to a recent report published by Price Waterhouse and Coopers, the live entertainment segment alone is poised to grow at 20 percent in the coming years.

e. Events as a Bonding Ground

B2B – Business to Business

These are events that are purely connecting businesses. These events are mostly aimed at allied business houses and the corporate. The requirement of B2B events can be defined as below:

- Manufacturing organizations that invite prospective vendor partners for raw material supply.
- Financiers inviting prospective Direct Selling Associates.
- Business houses in allied industries vying for joint ventures and partnerships.

B2B is also called as Institutional Alliances and events are customized to meet the requirements of these businesses. In general, these events feature a set of products of products and solutions for the invitees to view and deliberate with the host.

A detailed planning, careful scrutiny of the products to be displayed and an event flow is designed to ensure that the objective of the event is met and the stakeholder's interests are protected. The case presented below is a manufacturing organization with a presence across continents. The objective was deliberation on new technologies and selected institutional stakeholders were invited for an exclusive preview of the products, solutions and the technology.

The event was a two-day showcase alongside discussions, symposium and technical paper presentations with a live demo of the technology. This kind of display illustrated below is the core "event management" designing for the B2B segment.

The display zone entrance and the registration formalities to ensure only invited guests are allowed

The display inside the expo room where the products and solutions were unveiled

B2C – Business to Consumers

These are initiatives that connect the business with the end user or the "consumer." These initiatives are primarily an exercise to reach consumers to create "awareness-interest-attention-sale." The products that usually adopt this promotion tool are those where "consumer experience" is the key in the decision-making process.

These initiatives are usually adopted and effectively executed in the following domains of business:

- Automotive promotions
- Jewellery and expensive personal wear category
- Fashion and Designer wear category
- Builders and property promotions
- Healthcare and accessories
- Interior designer solutions

These initiatives are very effective as the end user or the consumer is equipped with all the necessary inputs that may be required in arriving at a decision. The "hands-on" experience allows the consumer to evaluate the pros and cons of the "offer" and have a window of opportunity to compare and deliberate with experts before arriving at a decision.

The consumer gets to see the product/service, evaluate the feedback from the peers and professionals in the trade, gets an exclusive preview into the services and is provided ample inputs to arrive at a decision. These initiatives are made memorable using the "promotion and experience" tools of Event Management.

The event designing that is deployed under these initiatives include:

- Designing a "virtual" experience or "simulation" experience zone.

- Unique "customer mapping" experiences.

- Template designed flow of "actions" to ensure uniformity in the "experience" for all guests.

- Surprise elements to entertain children who accompany the invitees.

- "Event memorabilia" for consumers before they depart.

- Special theme-based props/brand collaterals that would improve the user experience.

"Living Room display for a brand of lighting"   *"Mobile Lounge" – taking the product to the customer.*

f. Event Management Perspective in India – The Promising Business it is perceived as

The corporate sector's disillusionment with conventional media as a result of the increased clutter, increasing investments and questionable efficiency has opened up a formidable space for event marketing. Event marketing allows an organization to steer clear of the clutter in traditional promotion route, and target the right audience by enhancing experiences vide an association with a particular event

                    The Art of Building Experiential Events

while ensuring the product or service is well registered in the mind of the target audience and hence resulting in sales.

In India, the event industry was estimated to be around 350 cr (INR 3.5 bn) at the turn of the millennium and is today poised to be around Rs 4500 cr (INR 45 bn) and has been projected to grow at a high rate peaking double-digit growth within a decade. The business, from being individual driven, is taking the shape of an organized industry with professional players and trained talents who contribute to areas like Conceptualizing, Planning, executing, auditing and integration of new technology into the experience sphere.

The purpose of event marketing is primarily to increase brand/product awareness, getting products/service information to the end user, identifying and connecting target markets, brand recall, customer care and relationship-building. With the increased clutter in the traditional media, corporates today are very precise on their expectations of "deliverables" from event marketing. The decision to conduct an event rests on factors like brand persona, a well-defined objective for doing an event, the kind of audience that needs to be reached, the profile of the end user vis-à-vis the brand. The results are tangible and real. There is ample opportunity to develop experience grids, customer mapping, and result evaluations, which will help attract highly qualified talent to this sunrise industry.

Associating as sponsors with events is seen as a brand building opportunity and helps spread awareness for a product/service. Events are today sponsored by many corporates who derive value for their brand from such associations. The sponsorships also entail building a network of dealers and partners, which is another benefit of sponsoring. The events offer ample scope for brand endorsements using celebrities, which increases footfalls as also visibility for events. It is a proven fact that celebrity-endorsed categories return higher value to the brands and thus a higher recall.

The concept of engaging in big events is fast becoming a reality; apart from ground events. The electronic media plays a pivotal role in building hype and awareness for an event and contributes significantly with televising the event, which garners visibility and increases the revenue for the industry as a whole. The role of events is further strengthened by the advent of online and digital promotions in reaching the relevant audience. But what needs to be done is a detailed engagement with a select set of the target audience in understanding the customer psyche, behavioural pattern, perceptions, and response mechanism to specific engagements, which will enable the building of highly successful product events.

The organized event industry is still at a nascent stage and hence there is an urgent need to form monitoring authorities, audit bureaus, and lay down broad working methodologies and scientific evaluations for result management. The event industry will become an integral part of the communication domain and will be seen as a definite while devising promotion and communication budgets.

g. The Challenges in the Event Industry

1. **The Taxes – direct and indirect:** These taxes directly affect the profit of an event a lot. Increase in the quantum of Tax is a component which directly affects the volume and hence the profit of the business. Small and medium sized businesses negotiate a cost, which is net, and expect the agency to absorb the service tax incidence, which affects the profitability.

2. **Site clearances, authority clearances and permissions:** These are issues which severely affect small events. There's a host of permissions that need to be obtained, which cause hardships in executing an event. Apart from the regular permissions from the government, there are licenses like the performance license, label rights etc. and these are charged as fee commensurate to the nature of the event and the guest count. These add up to the event cost and finally depletes the profitability and hence leads to cost cutting.

3. **Talent and manpower:** Being the upcoming industry it is, there is a dearth of qualified, skilled and talented work force availability. There is an urgent need to create a pool of talent through intensive training programs that would meet the growing need of the industry.

4. **Corporate sponsored events:** These are events done specially for corporates to increase their exposure. These are easy as the objectives are defined, the requirements are mapped and the deliveries are monitored. However the agency is at risk when logistics, venues involved and the agency becomes responsible for any failure caused by other partners.

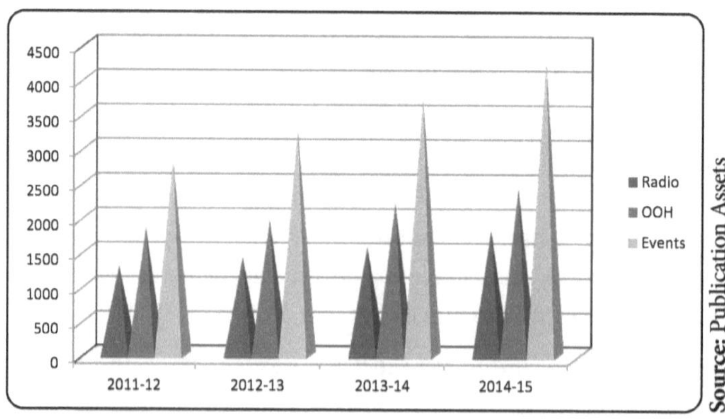

The Art of Building Experiential Events

5. **Brand sponsorship:** Public events are very promising for this industry as it assures work for many stakeholders, the biggest challenge lies in procuring sponsorships, which is largely dependent on numerous factors.

6. **Lack of venue and logistic facilities:** Identifying ideal venues is on one hand an issue, at the same time, availability of suitable venues for events and expos is a big challenge for the industry. Likewise, logistic management and connectivity for tier 2 and tier 3 cities also pose a challenge for the industry in expanding at a faster pace.

7. **Audit and rating successes:** Brands are increasing their spending on experiential marketing and are closely monitoring the return of value for their investments. The firm belief that events can return direct sales and exposures are prompting many corporates to look at events as a viable option for their investments. If the return on their investments could be monitored and shared in an audit format, the investments from brands will see a steady increase. As the event types are numerous (as detailed in the subsequent part), the audit and measuring formats need to be developed with customization and mapping the success of each event poses another challenge.

8. **The new age promotion tools:** The online and digital promotions at times pose a challenge to the event industry. The activation space of the event industry needs to necessarily include online promotion into their sphere of business to ensure good response. Else, the activation part can face a severe downslide of opportunities.

9. **Rising cost:** As the industry itself is just about growing, the stakeholder's behaviour pattern is that of "quick success" In short, the rates of venues, performers, and support like sound and lights hire etc. are directly proportional to the season and the location. There is limited price parity and this affects the model of the industry at large.

10. **Interface with social media:** The availability of social media is a boon and the event agencies depend heavily on the social platforms to drive event participation. The use of social media also helps in monitoring response.

11. **Technology:** With the advent of smart phones and apps, events need to quickly adapt them to offer measurable solutions with the right deployment of technology, else the event industry can see a decline in the volume of business.

12. **Unorganized market players:** This being a relatively new field, numerous players with short term vision and with less understanding of the business

dynamics enter the field offering prices cutting corners which affects the brand of the business.

13. **Vendor partnership:** The empanelment of vendors, are a critical factor in determining the success of event management. The major part of the industry still being unorganized provides abundant opportunity while, many new vendors do not understand the concept, the importance of execution and the process, which leads to substandard solution. Development of reliable, ethical vendors is another challenge this industry faces.

Challenges are to be viewed as a catalyst to overcome demotivation.
Seldom one views challenge as an opportunity.
The minute one is in realization of this,
there opens progressive opportunities.

– Deepak Swaminathan

Chapter 2
TYPE OF EVENTS

a. Music and Public Entertainment Shows

These are shows that involve the public audience, these are categorized as "entertainment" shows and are part of community celebrations, festival shows, standalone musical nights, and artistes performances. These are usually ticketed shows or sponsored shows. The performances are regional in nature and are specific in entertainment quotient to the location/zone/state they are performed in.

The above is an illustration of a show done under the category of musical entertainment event, which is typically a sponsored or ticketed show. Here, the guests attend either by purchase of an entry ticket or by way of donor passes extended by the presenting sponsor. The objective of these shows is primarily entertainment.

b. Corporate Recognition Programs

These are events that are customized specifically to a need and a requirement. The corporate programs are aimed at their employees to recognize their efforts, or are designed for the product or operation teams. These programs are not open to the public and the corporate decides the invitees and select guests from within the closed group. These events are funded by the corporate and the event team works in alignment with the corporate.

The above is the illustration of an event for a corporate. Here the guests are members of the designated corporate and the objective is well-defined and no deviation is entertained. The guests assemble for a specific purpose of recognition and the event is managed with a clear timeline and deliverables.

c. Dealer/Channel Partner Incentive Programs

These are classified as marketing events, which are aimed at recognizing the splendid work executed by the dealer or channel partners of the corporate. These events are usually outbound and are held at different locations each year. These events, are very detailed in nature and involves extensive planning, micro managing and efficient handling of the event and the special guests. These are also termed as marketing incentive events. The event is planned after every financial year and the best performing partner/dealer is invited for the recognition/incentive program.

The event in this category needs to align with the corporate brand objective, understand the profile of the guests and evolve special experiences that would enthral and motivate them to work more closely with brand and cement the relationship for betterment of business.

d. Sports Event

These are either public or private events. These events receive great attention and handling; these events require special experience in managing large crowds,

The Art of Building Experiential Events

planning for contingencies, complete alignment to safety and security and more than precise time management skills. These events are largely sponsored and are also televised. The event team needs to encompass all the requirements like permissions, team management, video recording, bouncer management, ticket sales management, visually appealing designs, F&B partners etc., which makes this event category complex yet highly challenging. Events like cricket tournaments, hockey, Grand Prix, soccer tournaments, snooker etc. fall under this category.

The above is a broad perspective of the largeness of this event and that provides a quick idea of the detailing and planning that go into making these events successful.

e. Marketing and Sales Conferences

These are also events that are corporate and brand specific. These are primarily aimed at the sales and marketing force of an organization and are designed to communicate the strategy, the plans and the brand roll out for the coming year. These events are spread over 2 to 3 days and the sales and marketing teams are invited to a residential conference wherein the event agency is expected to design awe-inspiring experiences to motivate the sales and marketing teams. These events feature product/brand salience presentations, technical specs of the products that are to be unveiled, case studies and entertainment is fused to motivate the teams. Some of these conferences also feature an awards event alongside this event to recognize the best performing teams and their leaders.

An ideal event of this category features a good mix of business and entertainment. Each corporate, depending on the budget, will request a variety of options to choose from. It is for the event agency to completely understand the requirement of the corporate and offer solutions that would enthral the guests and fit the budget.

f. Employee Engagement Programs

These are events designed for the human resource department of an organization. These are done as a "motivation" for the employees. There are set of objectives that would be put forth by the human resource department and these objectives will have to be met through these events. Some examples would be "teamwork"; "goal setting"; "crisis management"; "adaptability" etc. The event agency will work closely with the human resource department to understand the core objective and will then design an experience that would meet the goals set by the department.

We designed an event using 'sport' as a tool to reach the objective of the human resource department. The teams were given an indoor session on the core objectives followed by a live experience.

g. Technical Symposiums

Symposiums are completely technical in nature and have very little scope for entertainment. Most of these events are for the engineering, medical and information technology sector. The events are primarily "knowledge sharing" sessions and an event team which does not grasp the fibre of the event will fail in delivery thereby spoiling the "WOW" spirit of event designing.

The Art of Building Experiential Events

The symposiums have a combination of technical papers, technocrat discussions, plenary sessions, and chair and co-chair thought sessions. The innovation that the agency brings to the event makes it completely an upscale experience. Quick turn-around, nil lag time, technological adaptations are some key factors that make these events successful.

h. Expos and Exhibitions

This category is primarily for the B2B and B2C segment of the business. Expos are the norm to meet the right target and focussed business objectives. Expos and exhibitions throw open a sea of opportunities for the business. The opportunities vary from meeting prospective vendors, customers, new business initiatives and joint ventures. Many expos specialize in building forums for the "buyer-seller" interactions, thereby facilitating sealing of business deals. Today, expos and exhibitions are professionally managed by an event agency which details inputs and offers end-to-end solution. Superior customer experience, professionally planned and executed events, and time-bound action plans make expos and exhibitions truly memorable.

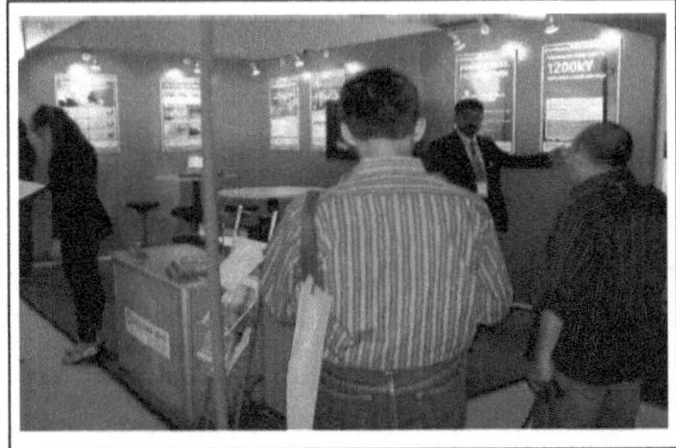

The visitors to the expos and exhibitions are predominantly from the allied businesses. Many a deals are finalized in expos and new business opportunities emerge for many of the participating companies. Expos are large events that entail many stakeholders and have a long gestation.

i. Weddings and Private Events

These are events that are primarily done for Individuals to celebrate an occasion like wedding, birthday or an anniversary. The scale and magnitude of the event is proportionate to the spending power of the individual sponsor. These are primarily customized to the taste of the sponsor family with focus on the colour schemes to be used, the type of props, the category of F&B partners, genre of entertainment and a selection of exclusive take away gifts. The role of the event agency here is restricted to offering solutions that please the sponsor and their families primarily. These events are scalable depending on the location, venue and the profile of the guests who are invited for these events.

A perspective of the Grandeur of an Indian Wedding

The above illustration depicts the grandeur of spend in designing and erecting a grand set in a thematic wedding/personal celebration. The above gives a preview of the ensuing expenses allied to the grandeur.

j. Social Cause Events

Designing events that have a connect to either raising funds for a charitable cause, or an event that is executed to promote a social message, or one that is specially designed to spread a message for the public audience is termed as a social event. These events are typically like the "marathon," "walkathon" "awareness camps" and "charity," type of events. Here, the focus is not completely like a business, but leans towards the charitable outlook. These events have gained immense popularity among the young and young at heart who generously contribute and also participate in them. The concept of such events arises from not for profit organizations and the event designing company engages from the "idea-execution" format to make these events memorable, and successful.

     The Art of Building Experiential Events

The above is a "marathon" event from a series designed and executed by the author through his agency promoting a cause. This event had a participation of over 2500+ runners with paid contribution and sponsorships.

k. Award Nite and Business Conclave

These are big ticket public events that are widely promoted, marketed and sponsored. These events are planned in advance, usually over a year. The events are executed around the same dates every year. These types of events usually involve a consortium of agencies that pan across categories (Online, On-Ground, Electronic, Print etc.). These types of events call for extensive planning, minute detailing and robust execution with "nil" error turn-around which makes these events highly challenging yet fulfilling. Examples would be film awards and business conclaves. Focus on safety, logistics, security and EHS adherences, are critical in making these events a success.

The ability to dynamically progress lies in the power of our mind.
The lesser the intent the slower the effort...
higher the intent the more powerful the effort.

– Deepak Swaminathan

Chapter 3

EVENT MANAGEMENT AS AN ESSENTIAL COMMUNICATION AND MARKETING TOOL

Event management and event marketing is considered as an important component by corporates, and separate budgets are allocated for spends. The events are conducted primarily in the area of customer connect programs, brand promotions, experience zones, activations, and PR exercises. The events are a means of connecting the brand owners with the end users.

a. Corporate Perspective of Event Management

Handling an event can turn out to be a challenge for the corporate if they intend to manage all aspects of the event by themselves as it requires a lot of time, energy and money. So, hiring a professional organization that is involved in handling such tasks is a sensible move. The corporates have pre-defined objectives and the very purpose for which they engage a professional event design agency is to gather the professional expertise that the agencies come with, which helps the corporate to focus on areas that would enhance their business opportunity.

Relation between corporate (business) and events

Creating an event to promote a business among the masses is a tried and tested method that can assist a company to gain attention as well as popularity. A successful event not only helps an established company to regain its importance in the customer's perspective but will also help a budding company to develop interest in its services among the public at large.

b. Channel Partner/Dealer Perspective and the Benefits

The dealer/channel partner who enagages a professional event agency are usually extremely cost sensitive and are keen to evaluate every dime spent on the activity. Many times, a badly planned event can result in limited objectives being met and the event can result in just collection of database, which may or may not be worthwhile.

Highly planned, and mapped event exercises offer tremendous scope for a brand/product to get high visibility and a great deal of mindshare. Customizing events to a specific target audience ensures importance for the guest also focussing on improving the customization, which makes the user experience a delight.

A micromanaged action plan with efficient teams and intelligently executed promotions will yield desired results. The dealers/channel partners will always look for quick results and this poses a challenge to turn the event around fast yet with measured spending.

Points that a dealer/channel partner will look for

Channel Partners Visibility: These are the last mile events that help the channel partner/dealer build value to his team towards achieving better results. These are termed as "brand activation" events and are run by the channel partner team with inputs and brand collateral support of the brand owner.

System and Process Driven: Time-bound action plans, process mapped execution, and robust systems ensure a successful event, and the partner is always keen in aligning these principles that are contributory factors for the success.

Holistic Solution: Ensure that the event is managed well, adhering to defined time line delivering superior experience.

Time-Bound Plan: A well-planned event brings in results immediately. Planning the invitees, the speakers, the dignitaries and ensuring the slots are well-lined and the content is well trimmed makes the event truly successful. Effort in planning a minute by minute agenda helps in running an event efficiently.

The Art of Building Experiential Events

Technology infused planning for better monitoring and positive results

Using latest technology ensures that reach the right target audience. With the advent of online and social media, effective use of this medium not only ensures good turn-out but also aids in delivering the right profile participation.

Post Event Connect: A robust reporting system which will help track leads back into the business, following up on delegates who attended, as well as generating latent interest from those who missed the event is another critical area.

Making the Effort Worth While: With deliverables mapped clearly, and with the use of monitoring software, the audit that is conducted post an event can be a great learning process, and also enables a continuous connect with the guests who attended the event.

c. Consumer Perspective

1. Who are they and what are they looking for?

With the advent of technology and numerous connecting apps, the profile of a consumer or a guest is well-mapped, so is the expectation of our guest. Many a sites are available to throw in the expectations as a consumer and quick responses enable a decision either for or against the participation. This is a boon to the organizers.

The guests today are specific of their objectives and expectations and it is in the interest of the organizer/event designer to ensure these expectations are met, and the fallout would be negative publicity if an expectation is not met.

Likewise, social platforms like Facebook, Twitter or LinkedIn commenced interest-based guest mapping. Social networks ask us lots of questions towards understanding the profile of expectations. As consumers, our tastes, preferences and our profile is out in the open domain for brand owners and marketers to reach us.

2. Search and its benefits

Until a decade ago search was the strongest area where Google and others revolutionised connect with end users. Keywords search was in vogue and this was resulting in a positive change but only until internet penetration was growing.

The current focus is more on trending and is influenced by the social preferences. Subconsciously the trends and social preferences guide the way decisions are taken.

We tend to spend time with like-minded people with whom we share similar thoughts. When a colleague decides to attend an event, it could give us insights into their needs and wants, thus influencing a decision. This could happen on many social networks. Today a requirement of a consumer is easily accessible through social networks.

In the coming years, with information of priorities available across domains, the consumer would greatly benefit from the information reaching them through intelligent networks and the consumer or the end user will have the choice to accept or reject it. Alternatively the consumer would be at an advantageous position to make his choices evaluating the abundant content available at their disposal.

The consumer will have a choice of options and will also have access on the profile of people attending an event/expo which would enable them to decide for or against the participation. Specially created "connect" sites would enable a preview of what can be expected by participating as also on the number of people who have chosen to attend and their profile.

Organizers have an opportunity to connect with prospects through blogs and personal notes shared online. These blogs can be snippets from the speakers or senior delegates which can attract positive participation from prospects.

The information sourcing is heavily influenced by post purchase. As a result, consumer experiences with events feed either **positive** or **negative** information.

3. Smart evaluation

The way consumers' source events have significantly progressed. Means that options and choices are easily available and accessible. The event websites also feature spaces for registering and sourcing details that would enable to form a decision.

This method makes a marketer's job tougher, mostly due to fragmentation of information. Correlating all the information available and deciphering them is many a times a shortcoming rather than an advantage.

That's why expert opinions and peer influence are even more relevant to make your event stand out. Inviting bloggers to your event may in fact slash down any non-reviewed alternatives.

4. Purchase cycle impact

There was a time in the past when the purchase was affected by the decision of peers and colleagues or our immediate kin, however the abundance of information

   The Art of Building Experiential Events

at command has resulted in a spurt of customized solution seeking, which has resulted in private thinking to arrive at a decision be it a purchase or participation. Many factors like post sales, service, consistency were all discussed prior to purchase, which has now changed.

If, as a participant, I hear something negative about an event I decided to attend, I would go on social media to check on the source of my information as also a validation which is available instantly and this would impact the decision while post decision contingencies could also be positive.

Creating live tweets, hashtags of events and ensuring trending champs be present in an event impacts building a trend for the event and the product so unveiled leading to reaching ideal target prospects who will help spread the word fast and economically too.

5. Post purchase experience

Irrespective of the evaluation feedback sheets that collected at site, the actual feedback happens concurrent to the event that is being staged. If a consumer/customer is unhappy with a product or a service, the feedback happens real time and in a matter seconds the word spreads across the target community. If the product/service registers an impressive performance this real time feedback is a boon.

In reality, the social networks spread the bad message faster than the good word and hence it is imperative to be cautious and at the same time well balanced before opening our doors to the world at large. The social networks enable consumers to take opinions, share feedback and at the same time decide the decision that need to be taken with regard to either a purchase or participation.

d. Employee Interventions

The employee of any organization views the events that are organized for them in 2 perspectives — 1. As a motivation for them by the employer; 2. As a random effort that he/she may need to necessarily participate in. In the existing scenario of perception, the events can be made entirely interesting and participative if the employee is able to identify himself/herself with any of the following.

1. Concurrent effort by the sponsor/management in building a "Value Proposition"

A one-off event invariably elicits a lukewarm response. The most effective way is to format the activity with clear time targets and build a momentum within the organization and make the event a looked forward to one which will increase the interest levels for the employees, thus improving the willingness to participate.

2. Equal representation of the employee and his peers

Many organizations repeat events, that are very predictable and features the same activities and performers which drastically reduces the interest for the employee to participate. An element of surprise, an element of change is very critical for the employee to represent and participate actively.

3. Recognition across all categories rather than just on performance at work

Recognition is a very important component for the employee to participate, the employee need to be convinced that the management recognizes not just one area but areas other than evaluating numbers and performances. This kind of evaluation is possible with the help of "image building" "communication building" events which improves the interest levels and thereby participation.

4. Day outings that would help enhance networking within the team

Employee intervention events are very effective in the "day outing" programs that are designed with specific objectives. A day outing program typically involves an external trainer, an event design team and an effective communicating moderator who apart from handling the "day outing" makes it essentially "corporate objective driven." These events involve many segments like "team plays"; "spot skits"; "games on themes"; "music jams sessions" etc. The employees identify such activities as a time to bond and network which increases their motivation and these events are looked upon as monotony breakers.

5. Special training programs that would aid in improving knowledge

Training is a very important intervention for the growth, sustainability and continued success of an organization. The benefits of training, becomes tangible on implementation. The efficiency and effectiveness quotient, increases progressively with the right training interventions. The right training increases the productivity of the trainee.

New incumbent employees who experience the right training interventions carry forward the vision, and the core fibre of the organization. This training intervention helps them understand and familiarize with the corporate mission, vision, ethos, culture, and the working.

The training is often part of intervention for the existing employees across levels. This helps in alignment to the concurrent requirements in tandem to the market dynamics which is ever changing. Training in technical areas help employees understand and adapt themselves to evolving methods and practices.

Regular training helps look at work from a different perspective and aids in improving deliveries and also gives immense satisfaction to the trainee/employee, which in turn reduces attrition.

e. Choosing the Right Event Management Organization (How the PARTNER Is Selected)

The moment a decision is taken to organize an event, the biggest question that emerges is "self help" or "look for a partner." It is never easy to map the complete process flow as events are made of numerous miniscule elements which if not addressed, can derail the entire activity. The decision to go alone or align with a professional agency grossly depends on the size, and the nature of the event that is being planned.

If the decision is in favour of hiring a professional agency, then it starts with a detailed "documentation" of what is the "outcome expectations" and a clear briefing of the objective, and end user profiles. If this document is not mapped well, then the outcome will definitely not match the expectations and will lead to a situation of "loss" both in values and costs.

The important thing to note is, if the event agency is professional, they would start by spending more time on the planning board with numerous sessions to discuss and iron out all points that would impact the final experience. The role of a professional agency would be to ideate, challenge, articulate, educate the client and ensure detailing is done to the last element, thereby ensuring that efforts are channelized towards one common goal, - "best experience."

Presenting below are parameters that help decide on "THE" partner who can design your event.

1. Map your requirements

Before engaging a professional agency, ensure that they have the requisite expertise that can meet your requirements.

Be ready with a description document that clearly spells out your expectations and the deliverables. It is also good to get a presentation from the prospective agency on their capabilities and bandwidth.

2. Due diligence of the prospective agency

With the event business being still unorganized, it is critical to understand the profile of the prospective agency, from the perspective of their existing clients, market feedback, reference checks, registration status of the company and also their tax compliances. Most of the engagements require the client to pay up an advance, and hence it is best advised to get satisfied on the agency profile before signing up.

3. The experience of the agency

Experience and expertise comes with a price. The more the experience and expertise the more is the price. With experience also comes the benefit of the event being in safe hands. Events are all about dynamic changes till the last minute. Even the most experienced and planned agencies are geared up for contingency management, which is acquired purely by the number of assignments and years they have been in business.

It is ideal to ask the agency to provide their client references and if it is possible also request a show reel presentation where you can get first-hand an experience of their execution capabilities. Requesting a presentation helps the client gauge the seriousness and confidence of the agency, likewise the agency also understands the intent of the client.

4. The 4 Ps in the event business – (People, Process, Planning, Passion)

With experience of over 2 decades in the business, the author strongly recommends the 4P principle which helps in bringing the client and the prospective agency closer to concluding a deal. Being meticulous, ethical and confident requires a great deal of perseverance, and if an agency is able to practice the 4P's consistently what brings about is a steady stream of new business, as also retain the existing clients.

When a client is sourcing an agency, apart from PRICE which is the most sought after quotient, there are 4P's which make a good agency. The Team (PEOPLE) make a big difference to the fibre of event that is planned and executed. The methodology (PROCESS), right from discussion stage till execution can be scientifically documented and executed. The Way one goes about (PLANNING) is an essential component which is the backbone of a successful experience, and an undying pursuit towards excellence (PASSION) goes a long way in retaining the spark that makes events memorable. Beyond any length of presentations and references, the client should have an eye for observing the presence of 4P's in an agency which if identified defines the agency to be appointed.

5. The associates and partners of the prospective agency

Many a times the event agency is likened to the "SOFTWARE" while their associates and partners are the "HARDWARE" part. If the software is robust but the required hardware is not aligned, be assured that the experience will definitely go wrong. Hence it is important to evaluate and discuss with the agency on their partner/associate strengths, their capabilities and turn-around capacity.

6. Cost and estimate arena

The spend levels, plays an important part of executing an event. Though the price should not be the most critical factor impacting a decision, it nevertheless crucial. If you are on a limited budget, remember that recruiting an economical agency does not always mean that the quality would be low. Proper understanding of the elements, categorizing their essentials and then drawing out the estimate can still ensure appointment of a professional agency at an economical price.

7. Keeping up commitment

This may not look important at the beginning of an event planning, but this needs to be planted and nurtured between the client and the agency from the first discussions. Agreeing in principle to deliveries, be it on commitments, disclosures, or payments. A well-established agency presents a docket that covers the above points which make them preferred partners.

Our clients are the most important & critical reason for us to be in business,
the more we cherish this relationship the more we are in business.

– Deepak Swaminathan

Chapter 4

QUALITIES OF PERSONNEL IN THE EVENT MANAGEMENT BUSINESS

a. Head of Business

The role as Event Head/Director is very important in the Business of Event Management and he/she needs to possess certain skills which are necessary, the key skills are:

- Communication
- Proficient Consultation Abilities
- Being a seasoned Team Player
- Planning and Eye for detail
- Logistics Management

Communication

This is the most important skill that a leader needs to possess, that is excellent communications. The ability to communicate effectively or in other words the ability to translate thoughts into an effective communication that would open up the opportunity with prospects.

Proficient consulting abilities

Another important task as Event Head is to constantly work at retaining good talent, and adding talent to the team. For identifying good talents, is required sound knowledge of the business, and good interpersonal skills. The head should be a person who can be looked forward to for any consulting. The leader should possess the ability to build a team that has the best mix of Experience, Knowledge and skills to manage the event successfully.

The head will need good consultation skills, working with the management team and with professionals at the associate companies as also with the last mile management teams.

In the business of events which is dynamic, more often the head may not possess the necessary skills to handle an event. But with an ability to consult with the right people and professionals, the head acquires knowledge which coupled with experience helps overcome shortcomings.

Being dynamic in nature, the business calls for a head/leader who would lead from the front along with his dedicated team to get the best output in a given assignment. The head/leader will win the team and also get to learn nuances by being on site and visiting partner facilities and connecting with all concerned with an event.

By working closely with the team, the head/leader gets insight into the capability of the team members and by winning their confidence will become a true mentor assigning responsibilities commensurate to the team player capabilities. This also helps in giving the right training to a team member to enable him/her perform well on their assignment.

Being a seasoned team player

Events require participation and support of a large contingent of team players and the number of members, keep adding as the event date comes closer. Depending on the nature of the event the number size of the team varies. There are events where there could be a minimum of 20 members involved and this can go up to 200 if the its large scale show or high profile event. The Event Head therefore has to effectively manage and deploy his team into roles where optimum results can be obtained. Event heads need "TEAM" skills and an innate ability to:

- Identify, and Recruit the right team that can deliver
- Plan and organize team meetings for planning and management
- Set objectives for the team to pursue
- Ensure unity and dependability among team members
- Consult professionals and team members to draw out event plan using their skills and expertise
- Delegate responsibilities and monitor performance of team members
- Help in ideating and validating workable solutions.
- Be a mentor to the team members and motivate them

Planning and eye for detail

The event planning for an event is not merely confined to a logistical acumen, it a complex set of factors that make an event successful. The journey from the discussion board to execution is complex, complicated and detail-oriented. However, with proper tools, methods and processes it is an easy and an enjoyable

The Art of Building Experiential Events

task. The eye for noting what need to be done and when it need to be done are 2 very important areas to be in control of. While it looks easy, the event planning agency need to live through the event well ahead of time to detail every possible challenge and issue and keep ready the plan for managing it effectively and also be ready with Plan B for all actions planned.

For example, getting and booking a venue is critical, and more critical is getting a venue that will suit the requirement. A failure in this area certainly prevents an event from getting forward. Likewise there are numerous tasks that need to be done at a specific defined time and order for the event to mature.

The Event Management team must develop a complete breakdown of all the tasks that need to be accomplished and accordingly plan for capable resources before allocating responsibility, timelines to ensure that the tasks are completed on time for the best outcome.

There are a number of techniques and tools available that will help in identifying and planning the completion of actions towards executing an event. The Gantt Chart is a popular and easy-to-use-technique for understanding the sequence and duration of tasks. Presented below is a chart that explains the first steps leading to an event execution.

No	Activity	Week 1	Week 2	Week 3	Week 4	Week 5	Week 6
1	Event objective	█					
2	Venue finalization		█	█			
3	Permissions and licenses		█	█	█		
4	Team allocation		█	█	█		
5	Branding formats		█	█	█		
6	Payout plans and advances			█	█	█	
7	Alliance partners			█	█	█	
8	Publicity and promotions			█	█	█	
9	Execution plan finalization				█	█	█

b. Client Servicing/Marketing

The role

The client service manager is the connect point between the agency and the client. This person is responsible for understanding the needs of the client and translating it into an effective execution by coordinating with the respective internal departmental heads.

They work towards developing strategies for the clients and works closely with the clients. In short, the client services manager is accountable for all aspects of the delivery of work to the client. But the role goes beyond merely giving a client what he wants. Client services managers act as solution providers who interact with clients, understand their expectations and analyse the challenges of the clients and help them develop implement promotions through events.

Their role

The role played by the client service managers is customized to the requirements of each client. Their daily tasks include providing the work in process, the progress reports on specific activities, submitting status reports, discussing with clients any inputs that they may need and coordinating with the necessary teams internally. Be it designing, operations or finance. The biggest responsibility of the client service team will be to retain the client and ensure cordial relations are maintained and providing quick solutions for the expectations set by the client.

Knowledge of business and industry is a necessity for this role, be it a manufacturing client or a hospitality client, the role demands being knowledgeable of the current trends in the industry. The demands can be as simple as getting a layout for a brand collateral to an activation project within a short time span. The success of the role depends on the trust they build with the clients and the reciprocation of the same.

Characteristics

The client services managers need to demonstrate effective work traits. They need to manage multiple clients, multiple requirements and be agile yet courteous. They need to be adept in manoeuvring changes of the marketplace. They're organized. People skills are also a must, as their role defines cross channel interface.

They are expected to be available as the need arises and need to possess the ability to manage pressure and maintain warm relationships with departmental heads. Being the face of the agency, the client service manager has to be warm and committed, polite yet firm and subtle yet convincing on issues both within the agency as also with the Clients.

C. Operations

The operations manager plays a pivot role in translating the requirements of the Client Servicing team, grasping the creative teams outing, managing the site cost expenses and ensuring that the deliveries match the needs defined by his internal customers (Client Servicing/Designing/Finance). The operations team are the front end warriors at site, who work under tremendous duress and are the receiving point of crisis and misses caused by any stakeholder.

Eventually the operations manager and his team are responsible for "On-time" delivery of an event, without compromising on any of the commitments specified by the client and his internal customers. If an event is successful the operations team also receives the appreciation along with his peers, but if the event goes wrong, the operations manager is in the line of fire.

The operation manager gets introduced post an in principle approval is given to the agency that they are on board to handle the assignment. The finer details of the venue/logistics/time plan/delivery schedules/resource planning/setting up the venue/dismantling plans are the key delivery areas of the Operations Manager.

A broad look at the responsibilities of the operations manager

- Meeting up the client coordinating team to understand critical requirements concerning the event

- A quick grasp of the agenda and gearing up for possible last minute requests

- A Grid chart of definite requirements, not so important & things that may not be required at all

- A document on the probable last minute requests the client may come up with.

- Discussion with client servicing and Finance teams on the costs that need to be billed for additionally for requirements that would have been missed by the client

- Presenting the Layouts/3D versions, contingency plans.

- Delivery plan with details

- Advising clients on critical Do's and Dont's that may affect the event

- Recommending partners who would be ideal for the conduct of the event

- Appraising the Finance teams on the permissions/licenses that may be required for a venue or an event genre

- Mapping and ensuring all EHS compliances are met with

- Personnel insurance, safety gears and health check for all site personnel

- Logistic plan encompassing arrival time, unloading, shifting of materials aligned to the ground rules of the City/Venue.

The qualification & skills

In India, we still do not have an organized set up to train talents for Event Operations, as most part of the learning happens through experience. However with the advent of Corporate into the business of Events, the expectations of Clients have increased phenomenally and hence the need for Qualified Operations team is becoming essential to compete and win assignments. The ideal operations Manager would possess the following

- Degree in Arts/Diploma in Construction

- Working Knowledge of Graphic design

- Passion for designing props

- Exposure to Art-Direction

- Passion to create props that are simple yet novel

- Team player with a high degree of patience

- Focus on challenges with an eye for quick solutions

- Calm yet firm personality

d. Designers in the Event Agency

The graphic designer is the person who converts words into illustrations, and hence need to have a keen ear on what the client demands. The graphic designer need to demonstrate a passion toward using colours, images, designs and should be able to turn-around even a dull brief into an attractive communication design.

A graphic designer works on a variety of requirements like spec cards, colour cards, branding collaterals, designs for social media, online designing, websites, brand dockets, exhibition display panels, event related designing etc. i.e. providing a visual identity.

The profile demands creative understanding, knowledge on latest designing tools and software, knowledge of industry and the current styles in vogue, and of course a firm eye on timelines and costs.

Responsibilities

The designer will be managing multiple clients and activities simultaneously and hence need to be on top of all situations to deliver to tight deadlines. The broad scope of responsibility include

- Meeting with client service team, account manager team and clients for collecting requirements
- Work closely with the Accounts department on the estimation of the work
- Understanding the client brief in full and offering time tested solutions
- Update self on newer technologies and trends
- Deploying new age solutions for optimizing spends
- Designing and adaptation aligned to the brand docket
- Presenting the work to the clients and seeking feedbacks
- Ensure proof read copies are shared with the client
- Ability to conceptualize and communicate to the client of an idea
- Managing set of page makers, caricature artistes, copywriters, and photographers

What to expect

- Design work commences with taking the brief and working on concepts and creative.
- The success rate depends on the appreciation heaped by a client for a design done well.
- They build a name for themselves with every work and accounts have often shifted along with the moving of a designer too.
- Although the work is mostly studio-based, travel within the working day to meet clients may be required.

Qualifications

Relevant subjects for graphic design work include those that involve visual arts. In particular, a degree or Diploma in Designing and knowledge in the following subjects are essential:

- Basic graphic designing knowledge
- 3D Animation and designing;

- 2D animation, cell animations
- Photography, film/television;
- Hand art and visual art.

Any design-based course will give a good start for a career in designing. Sound knowledge in the latest of software, systems and free hand drawing helps in developing stunning designs. Apart from the qualification, there need to be an inborn love for developing creative designs which is the fountain of development in career. A high degree or a postgraduate qualification isn't necessary, however experience counts with picking up the right knowledge while on the job.

Skills

Apart from technical and drawing skills, you will need to show:

- Passion for creating wonderful designs
- Working under pressure
- Adaptability to client requirements
- Adhering to deadlines
- Being good at cost estimation
- Excellent communication and Interpersonal skills
- Ability to translate an idea from a discussion stage to an action stage
- Attention to detail and finesse in designing
- Willingness to take negative comments and build on positive ones

e. Safety Head

The safety head is a well-experienced person with experience in Environment, health, Safety and Security with a relevant qualification from a reputed university and is expected to possess a track record of having handled events of different scale. The safety head offers time tested solutions while strictly adhering to the safety norms put down by Governing council.

Key points health and safety management include

- Drafting a customized health and safety policy.
- Training and Enabling practice of the safety policy so designed.
- Ensuring strict adherence to the safety policy.
- Training teams and Recording deviations.

- Close monitoring of the effective implementation of the policy.
- Planning and conducting audit of the implemented policy at regular intervals.

The role of the safety head

- **Stage 1 – *At Commencement:*** At the time of identification of the venue, validation of the venue from the perspective of safety, the equipment that would be used, their design approvals, selection of competent workforce, discussions with vendor/partners and selection based on pre-set criteria.

- **Stage 2 – *During Progress:*** Ensuring that all safety parameters are evaluated, validated and are being adhered to. The safety head will own up to question any deviation on the promised criteria.

- **Stage 3 – *Pre-Event Final Round:*** Inspection of all fitments and equipment, stability checks, electrical circuit safety, venue safety and emergency assembly points. The safety head will also be responsible for the safety and security of the workmen and delegates of the event.

- **Stage 4 – *D-Day:*** Ensuring all round safety across event venue—that covers the set up, the entry and exit, parking, guests, F&B zone, transport and logistics and VIP management. The safety head will also be responsible to implement, monitor safety posts at the event venue to handle a sudden crisis.

- **Stage 5 – *Dismantling and Safe Exit:*** The safety team works post the event to ensure safe dismantling of all equipment and also ensures safe passage of the materials and crew that were involved in the execution of the event.

- **Stage 6 – *Deviation Mapping and Auditing:*** The safety officer will conduct a safety evaluation meeting involving all stakeholders and will present the observations, appreciations and deviations if any. The safety head also has the authority to black list a partner if found to have violated the safety norms.

Risk assessment – 5 step method *(safety planning for events.)*

1. List down the areas of focus for implementing safety procedures and map the extent of risks

2. Sync the risk areas with the stakeholders who would be involved In the same

3. Implement the check points for safety adherence

4. Train all team members appropriate to the level of risk exposure

5. Implement and Monitor

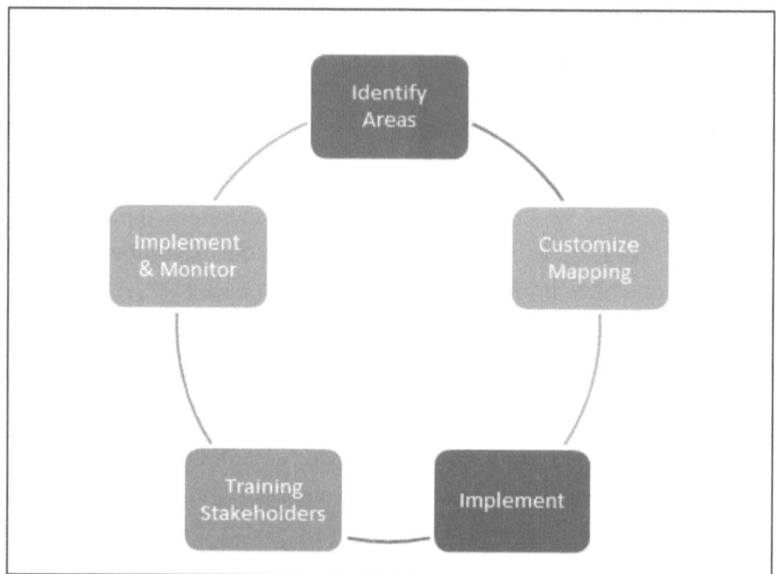

The entire activity will be documented from the word go with the initials of all stakeholders, their training, solutions for any challenges, their performance at site, observations and corrections and all deviations will be captured. The above is a good practice and if adhered to well, then it implies that the safety parameters have been well appointed. Safety is the utmost important component and any compromise can lead to a situation of unrest in the event of an eventuality.

f. Logistics and Site Coordinator

If the materials and crew are not reaching on time for a set up or for an event, the team responsible for the same is the Logistic and Site Coordinator. This team comprises of experienced professionals from the logistics management sector. Primarily they are the nerve point between the agency office and the site. This Logistics and site coordinator plan, and organize the delivery of good and safe keep at the venue. The role demands high focus on job as a wrong delivery can cause both financial as also brand damage. This team would ensure the right props, equipment are delivered at the right location at the right time at optimum cost. Concept of the supply chain is critical to effectively coordinate with stakeholders and consumers.

Roles and responsibilities

- Ability to assimilate all supports that would be required for an event

- Close monitoring and understanding of the specific requirement of a prop/team/equipment at site

- Effective use of Information technology to monitor and control crisis
- Instruct, Coordinate and track movement of requirements aligned to the need at site
- Plan and ensure all clearances are obtained at site prior to the materials and crew from reaching a venue
- Discuss and negotiate with customers and suppliers;
- Pre-empt areas of challenges, plan back-up and effectively overcome situational challenges
- Work on cost optimization which will improve the profitability of the agency
- Strict adherence to safety procedures and its effective implementation
- Training and Motivating team players
- Project management
- Identify new partners to improve operational efficiency
- Use specialist knowledge, such as mechanical-handling systems, to provide consultancy services.

Skills of the logistics and site coordinator

- Coordination skills
- Team management and crisis management ability
- Work with clear action planes
- Ability to foresee issues and come with real time solutions
- Decision-making ability
- Good at expense management
- Knowledge of logistic software
- Be flexible and have the ability to manage change;
- Possess good interpersonal skills and have the ability to work well as part of a team.
- Have excellent communication skills, both oral and written;
- Be able to negotiate and use your analytical skills.

g. Accounts, Finance and Taxation Manager

The Accounts, Finance manager articulate every assignment to the last detail of fund requirement and spending and advice the management on the viability of each assignment. This role demands, a dynamic person who is good in numbers and possess the ability to decipher requirements and expectations into numbers. The manager should be good at analysis, data compilation, should be creative in optimizing expenses and improving bottom lines. They prepare weekly, monthly, quarterly and annual performance reports and help the organization to be on path of profit at all times. The role is highly demanding and can be highly pressured too as they may need to organize funds on a short notice, manage pay outs without derailing the system. Accounts, Finance and Taxation managers work on the following:

- Revenue and Expenditure sheet for each assignment.
- Financial audit reports.
- Performance reports for each cost centre.
- Legal compliance reports and documents.
- Payables and Receivable management.
- Statutory compliances and tax pay outs.
- Taxation details and remittances as per the Law.
- Plan, and implement innovative ways to reduce costs.
- Empanel Funding partners and manage finance and rise up to an occasion.
- Advice Management on business health and help them take financial decisions.

With the advent of technology, the managers have at their command access to voluminous data which can be effectively analysed using latest technology to accurately pin point profitable actions and non-profitable actions. The technology has greatly helped in compressing the time required to prepare reports that earlier used to take months.

The Accounts, Financial responsibility also include negotiating rate cards with vendor/partner sign MOU with empanelled partners that would include quality assurance, delivery assurance, payment assurances and credit terms that may be mutually agreed. The role demands a professional advisory status to the management in advising them on critical decisions which will impact the business prospect. The manager also works closely with fund managers and bankers and maintains a very cordial relationship which is important for a business to thrive and sustain. They have to align with the laws of the state in filing the necessary reports and ensuring that compliances are met in complete.

Skills and qualification that are looked for in accounts, finance and taxation manager

- A Graduate in Commerce and Finance, with a Post-Graduation or a specialization in Finance planning and audit.

- Interpersonal skills and ability to manage pressure and deliver in trying times.

- Analytical skills and ability to understand numbers in the context of business and read through them to provide intelligent solutions.

- Excellent communication skills, ability to understand and interpret financial transactions.

- Attention to detail. Quick to prepare financial reports and Balance sheets and Income Expense statements.

- Knowledge and understanding of international finance and legal documentation.

- Abreast of the latest laws, bye laws in Finance and Taxation.

- Manage excellent Client-Vendor-Team relationships.

Transparency is a wonderful virtue and when we club it with our innate experience, the output is just DIVINE.

– Deepak Swaminathan

Chapter 5

THE ART OF PRESENTING THE EVENT ORGANIZATION

The opportunity to present an event organization/agency is positive welcome for the marketing team. It's a window to present a strong case of the agency profile and if articulated well, this first opportunity can turn into a permanent business association. With an experience of close to two decades in pitching and promoting an agency, the author has evolved a 7 spoke model which has been effective in winning orders and further right steps had ensured continued association with many a leading corporate.

Before presenting the model, few tips while pitching that one need to keep in focus are:

- Be Precise and simple
- Correlate similar assignments as a gist
- Keep the pitch short
- Eye contact with every member of the client team
- No False Information or Name Dropping unnecessarily
- Make the flow like a story
- Touch on challenges and ability to overcome.

The 7 Spoke Model (Developed by the Author)

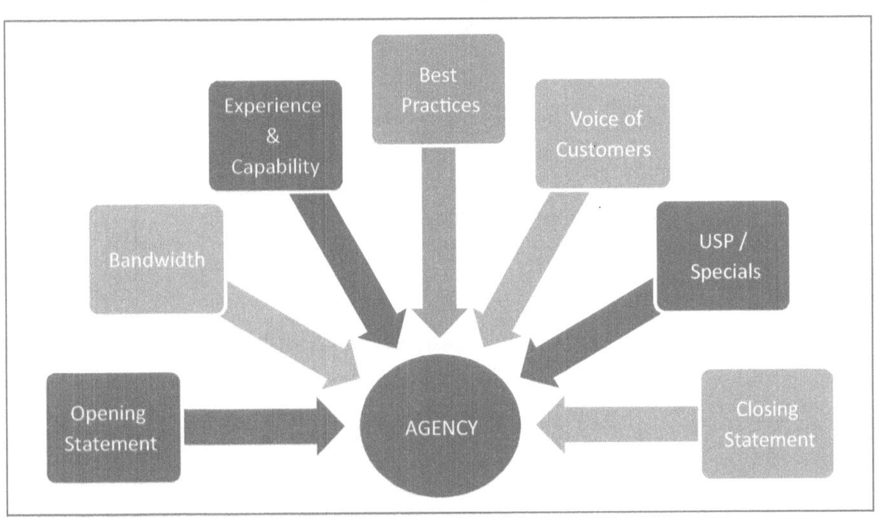

a. The Opening Statement

Presented below is an evolved, tried, tested and a successful style of Introducing the Agency (the details provided herewith are the facts of the Author's Organization – Media Point)

We thank you for the valuable time given to us to present our organization. We take pleasure in presenting about our agency and the pride works that we have executed till date.

We are a professionally managed event design and management agency headquartered in Chennai, India with a pan India presence and partner presence in South East Asia and Middle East.

We commenced its operation in 1998, and today has a pride of having handled 4000+ events across countries. We have trained manpower, specialized design personnel, skilled technicians and able managers who ensure that our events are planned to the last detail leaving no stone unturned.

We take pride in sharing some key facts about us:

- Established in 1998 In India.
- Headquartered in Chennai.
- Pan India Presence.
- Representations across GCC, SEA, Sri Lanka.
- 4000+ events Across India, Sri Lanka, Africa, GCC, SEA, Turkey.
- Process driven system.
- End-to-End Service Provider for our clients.
- Associations span over five years with each of our clients.
- We believe in working truly as an extended arm of our clients.
- Prompt and Reliable deliveries.
- Time tested solutions.
- Complete hands-off experience for our clients.

b. The Bandwidth

With a presence across Metros and Mini Metros in India, we have access to the whole gamut of services that would be expected of a professional event design agency. The following details the bandwidth of our organization.

- Event Conceptualizing, Planning, Execution and Management
    - Global Seminars and Meets
    - Product Launch
    - Corporate Conference
    - Employee Day Celebrations
    - Awards Nite
    - Entertainment (Celebrity, Theme Based and General)
    - Expos and Stall Construction
- Design Solutions [Corporate, Theme and Event]
- Web Portals
- Promotions – End-to-End Solutions [BTL]
- Corporate Film
- Press Relations and management

c. The Experience

We present below our expertise and experience which is a factor of the varied genre of events that we have designed and handled. Media Point commenced its operation in 1998, and today has a pride of having handled 4000+ events across countries. Our expertise, include:

- Branding and Designs: Strict adherence to brand guidelines, yet offering innovative designs and price sensitive solutions has been the hallmark of our designs.

- Corporate Films and AV: Customized solutions deploying the latest techniques fused with special effects and creating unique visual master pieces that are "All Media" friendly has won us many a prestigious assignments. Our expertise evolved over 100+ Films delivered by us.

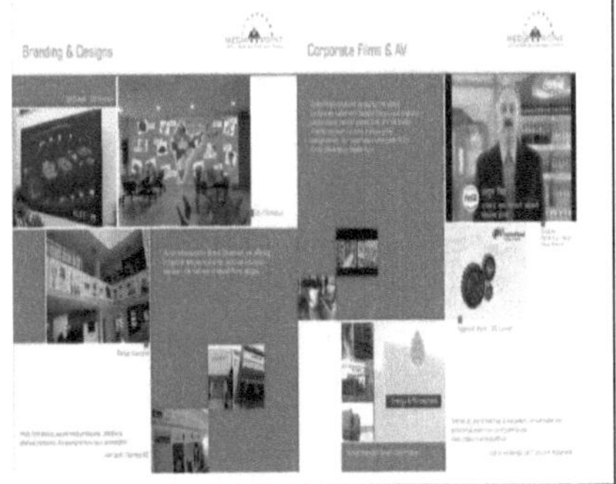

- Exhibitions, Road show and Social: With complete understanding of the core objectives, our teams design, produce and manage exhibitions, Road shows (India and Global) and social events with a firm control on the guest delight element.

- Symposium, Award Nite and Recognition Programs: Stylish Production, Top of line visual experience, Technology fused entertainment, and vibrant program management has been the "Mantra" for the dynamic team at. Over 2000+ shows in this genre have given us a privileged pedestal and we work tirelessly to maintain the lead.

- Product Launch: Each of our designing leaves a unique experience, from consumer products, to automobile from hospitality brand to Engineering from Information technology to Telecom, we believe that innovation and experience are the core pillars to build these events. Our events are designed to leave positive lasting memories.

The Art of Building Experiential Events

- Facility inauguration: Sensitive, is how we define these events. Detailing, multiple check points, fail proof systems, numerous runs, engaging with our customers, time tested deliveries and the awe-inspiring concepts and solutions, gives us a sense of accomplishment after each inauguration. Media Point has had the unique privilege to have inaugurated many state-of-the-art green field facilities pan India.

- Photo Shoot and e-Souvenirs: The art of Imagination is best expressed though images, we believe in bringing alive memories of "Special Moments" through our "Photo Shoot" and "e-Souvenir" solutions. A dedicated team of professional creators from our agency blend the "real" with a touch of "Magic" that weaves "Joy and Nostalgia."

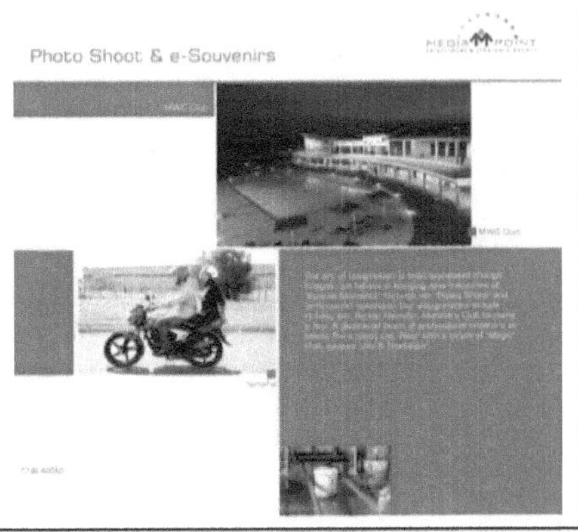

- Theatre, Entertainment and Family Day Our Love for country, ignited in us the passion to create and present special musical theatre on India and its Enviable Heritage.

  Our agency has produced over 10 widely recognized musical theatre on India which has showcased in many International and Domestic events.

- International Expositions: Our agency had been elected for four consecutive editions to be the Event Partner of a Global Expo. A biggest show of the Power Sector. The inauguration and all concurrent events are held back to back and a strong understanding, planning, detaining, execution and management is the key for the success of our agency in these assignments.

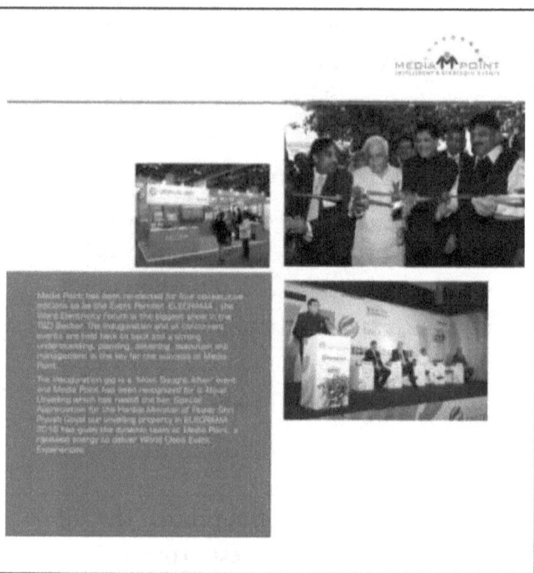

d. The Best Practice Compliances of the Agency

The agency has to present their credentials with complete honesty and ethics. It is in the interest of the Agency, Client and the Event that paramount importance is given to the Environment, Health and safety issues while planning and designing an event. Every event has an objective and it involves a wide spectrum of audience who are critical for the success of the event. Hence it is very important for the event design agency to plan and commit itself to the best practices which will increase the success rate of an event while earning repeated business.

Listed below is a sample of the Best Practice compliance that defines the quality of performance.

- Safety of our workforce

    - All workforce (both direct and indirect) are covered under WCP

    - We ensure proper and safe transportation of the Workforce at all times

    - Adequate Health Insurance is taken for all the workforce at site

- Safety at work site

    - All Workmen involved in Risk exposed activities are provided with safety shoes and helmets

The Art of Building Experiential Events

- Warning gear with safety belts are provided to Workers at Height
- No Hazardous chemicals or loosely fitted tools are allowed at our work site
- Electrical related works are handled only by trained and experienced workforce

- Equipment handling and management
  - All heavy equipment are shifted using trolleys and capable workforce
  - Electrical units and sound and lights are only with German sockets
  - No taping of wires/joining of wires are allowed by our management
  - All vehicles have proper documents (Pollution control, Valid Road tax, Insurance and valid licenses.)

- Workmen profile
  - All workmen are over the age of 18
  - Strict adherence to the attire is maintained and deviations are not entertained
  - No liquor or smoking at site
  - All workmen carry name tags/badges and their rooster is maintained by the Site manager

- Human factor
  - Our operation plan encompasses the Human Factor in all our workings at site for our Workforce as also for our clients and their guests

e. Voice of Customers

Every pitch need to showcase "The Voice of Customers," as this subtly validates the submission of the agency. The Voice of Customers gives the pitch credentials that help the new client to decide in favour of the agency.

It is smart to carefully plan the choice of "Testimonials" that are presented during the pitch. A successful agency gets appreciation from their clients and these need to be recorded vide a video byte or vide a written note. The more the events, the more the number of "Testimonials" that can be presented.

Providing testimonials from allied businesses or established business houses gets the notice in a pitch and it answers many questions on capability, bandwidth, dependability etc. for the new client.

f. Voice of Pride

The "Voice of pride," is a careful selection of "Milestone" events that have been designed and handled by the agency. This is used to counter any query that the client may raise on the "Profile of Events" handled, the capability of the agency to manage challenges, the "Sensitive" events that the agency may have designed and handled.

The Voice of Pride is a presentation of "High Profile" and "Sensitive" events that have been designed and executed by the agency. The events that feature here need to cover and detail the following:

- Consistency in being in the circuit
- One stop shop solution providing
- The title of events
- Relationship reflecting assignments
- The nature of the events
- The size of the events
- A notable remark on the Fibre of the event
- A footnote on the Agency Responsibility

This part of the presentation can swing the decision of a prospective client in favour of the agency. A careful compilation of the "Pride" events can be presented in one of the following formats for effective acceptance.

- A Table of events with reference of the Years as a growing model
- Pictorial presentation with details of event sensitivities
- A show-reel of the special assignments and the accolades as a Voice over
- An interesting caricature like a collage

g. The Closing Statement

We appreciate your business, and if we are assigned this opportunity, we assure you an event that would be memorable, effective and truly a best in class experience. Thank YOU!!

A client engages an agency with a hope of getting the best solution, and it is our foremost duty to educate the client to an optimum point that would enable build an unshakable trust.

– Deepak Swaminathan

Chapter 6

UNDERSTANDING THE CLIENT AND THEIR EXPECTATIONS

a. Type of Clients

The types of clients are many, but for the purpose of this publication, we shall classify the clients into 3 broad categories. Most of the clients fall under one of the category mentioned herein. Though the types of clients vary their broad objective may not be in large variance.

The client categories are:

- Corporate clients (business houses)
- Associations or Not for Profit Organizations
- Sponsors of public events like musical shows/theatre shows etc.

b. Their Objective and Expectations

Corporate clients

These clients primarily are registered organizations, with presence in more than one city and have a name for their products and services. The events for the corporate clients are broadly done for the product promotion, employee engagement, inauguration of a facility, branding/product introduction programs for their channel partners etc.

Association or not for profit organizations

These are industry associations that are the apex bodies representing a category of business, for example the Power Association, Chemical and Drugs association, Plastic association, Paint Association etc. These apex bodies function as a bridge between the industry and Government agencies in leveraging their collaborative strength of the industry in influencing the policy making and guiding the Government by providing accurate and reliable information about the industry, the performance, the challenges.

The association is represented by the industry leaders who hold office for defined period and the leadership changes after the defined period. These associations hold events to showcase the industry and create business opportunities for the members and the category at large.

Sponsors of public shows like musical shows/theatre shows etc.

These are primarily the public shows which are arranged by a promotion company, or by Charity organizations that roll out these initiatives to raise funds for a cause. Typically these are classified as public events and these may either be ticketed events or sponsored events.

If the show is sponsored then the sponsors would have their expectations spelt out and the same need to be captured well while designing the event. The event will have single or multiple sponsors and each sponsor will have their demands to promote their product alongside the event.

It is the duty of the event designer to collate the requirements of each sponsor, work in tandem with the communication department of the sponsor and arrive at the best promotion solution for the sponsor's products/brands and execute the same without disturbing the core objective of the event.

The requirements of each of these clients are different and for effective designing of the event, it is imperative to identify objective, define the corner stones and expectations for designing the event.

c. Questions to Frame Client Expectations

From the vast experience in designing events, the author has designed a typical format of points that are discussed in the first meeting to arrive at the event objective and expectation. These questions are not shared in a printed format to the client during the discussion but are on a dialogue mode to understand the expectations.

No	Question/ deliberation points	Corporate clients	Associations	Sponsor events
1.	What is the event about	Product launch	Exhibition	Musical show (Film Music Nite)
2.	When is it scheduled	Next month	In 3 months	In 6 months

　　　　　　　The Art of Building Experiential Events

No	Question/ deliberation points	Corporate clients	Associations	Sponsor events
3	Which city	Mumbai for the first event and subsequently to 2 other cities	Bangalore	Chennai
4	Venue	Agency to recommend	Expo centre	Agency to recommend
5	Number of guests	500 pax	150 stalls and 3 events each with a guest count of 1000	Targeting 5000 attendees
6	Guests detail	Dealers/ marketing and sales personnel of the company	Member corporate, B2B delegates Government heads Business visitors	Family audience Music enthusiasts Press guests Celebrities
7	Objective of the event	A new product to be unveiled, sales team and dealers to be charged and motivated	Category visibility Business opportunity International visitors Strengthen business ties	Fund raising for a charitable trust that supports specially challenged Children.
7a	Has this type of event been done by the client before	Yes, we do this kind of exercise once in a year and we were not happy with the outcome	This is a bi-annual event and is a highlight of the industry, the scale has gone	No, this is our first attempt in doing a show of this scale. We need complete hand holding

No	Question/ deliberation points	Corporate clients	Associations	Sponsor events
		of the earlier event done by an armature agency	up so are the expectations. Hence we are looking at an established agency	by the agency in helping us put the thought together and support in designing and executing this show
8	Timing of the event	09:00–22:00	10:00–18:00 For 3 days	19:00–22:00
9	Preferred venue type	Indoor Banquet in a 5* Hotel	Hanger to be erected	Open air
10	Broad requirements	Dais, backdrop, new age projection sound, lights and entertainment, host, photo and video, award, special videos, cocktail and dinner and closing DJ	Stalls, venue branding, security, permissions, illumination, event Management, VIP protocol, floral décor, bouquet, registration at site, stall support	Permissions, branding, sponsor coordination, designing of props, barricade, side walls, high end sound light systems, venue lights, celebrity identification and management.
11	Choice of entertainment	The product being a wellness product, request the agency to advice	Prefer the agency to suggest a fusion based program or a choreography that would suit the occasion	Need a celebrity based band that is a crowd puller and tickets need to sell fast and sponsors should also come forward to invest

No	Question/ deliberation points	Corporate clients	Associations	Sponsor events
12	Profile of guests	All India dealers, and all India sales and marketing personnel, top management of the organization	International and national delegates, business owners and heads of large corporations, indian government delegates and international government delegates	City specific, regional audience, family audience with an interest in film music and celebrity singer following fans
13	Invitation/ Promotion Plan	Personalized invitations, reminder through groups online, hand holding support from the sales team	Press meets, ads in dailies, hoardings across host city and at metros, online promotions, road shows across cities to popularize expo. Government supported event, hence protocol road shows will be required	Barter deals for promotion partner, print and electronic media promotions, ticket sales from popular hangouts, posters in popular malls and venues, online promotions, sponsor deals and promotions through sponsor outlets

No	Question/ deliberation points	Corporate clients	Associations	Sponsor events
14	Theme that the client suggest	A thought that communicates the spread and intensity of the commitment of the brand and respect for treating our dealer partners as our own arm	"Powerful India" The thought behind the expo is to explore the vision of the government in building smart networks and improving the power generation of the country	"Gaana for YOU" This is a pure fun event and we want our guests to come and chill out at the venue, with an evening to remember and celebrate as they dance to the tunes that have entertained them
15	How soon would be finalizing the event design and management partner	We would need to finalize the partner in a week's time as the event is scheduled in one month's time	We are already late and we should finalize within the next 2 weeks to commence the ground plan and works	We are not looking at any other partner, but you as we have got very good feedback from the market on your capability and bandwidth
16	The criteria for agency selection	Establishes, good bandwidth, reference of similar product launches are mandatory, concept is key to decide, and industry references,	Prior experience in handling such shows, innovation in the expo unveiling, large team of professionals, credentials of the registered	Agency to support in getting sponsors, identifying the venue and support at all areas, continuous knowledge interventions required, payment for

No	Question/ deliberation points	Corporate clients	Associations	Sponsor events
		agency and a complete tax compliant agency. Selection is also based on vendor empanelment that meets our criteria	agency, bank guarantee, operation document to be submitted on in principle confirmation. No advance and payment only after the event.	agency s only from sponsor source and the promoter would not be able to pay anything till they collect advances.
17	Approximate idea on the spends	We are looking at a competitive price.	INR 10 Mn	INR 6 Mn plus taxes
18	Short comings if any of the previous editions	There were technical issues during the earlier launch, detailed planning was missing, the hotel room coordination was not done well, the overall planning had many challenges and the company teams had to step in to manage the issues. The awards were delivered late.	We were happy with the earlier agency, however since we have now enlarged the scope and scaled up the size of the expo, we have decided to look at a larger agency commensurate to the current size of the expo	Since we have not done this kind of an event earlier, we completely rely on the strategy and intelligence of the agency t support and guide us in making g this musical Nite a memorable one

d. Interpretation of Client Thoughts

The above set of questions is primarily the probing meter to help take a decision with regard to the presentation the agency needs to make. By following a professional dialogue format, the agency can pin down the exact issue that the clients worry about and hence can propose ideas and innovations that would amply cover the challenging areas. The fundamental purpose of engaging an event design and management agency is to get the professional expertise, most agencies fail to realize their role and perform duties typically like a supplier. The moment the agency team realizes and aligns itself to the common objective/goal of the client, the solutions fall in place quickly and magically and the result would be beyond expectations.

No	Interpretation grid	Corporate clients	Associations	Sponsor events
1	The role of the agency	The role is a supportive one. The client is well aware of their requirements. The agency needs to do their job professionally and offer the clients a hands-off experience. An inclusive role is what will be expected of the agency.	The role demands high participation. Expectations would be very high. The agency will play a role of an insider as also an external resource. Smart selling is key.	The role here demands high involvement. The agency will have to provide continuous and holistic support. Many a times the income may not be commensurate to the efforts.
2	Constraints	Their mind frame towards agencies caused by their previous experience. High level of interference can be expected as client has been	A conscious decision to go to a bigger agency will be the benchmark in all discussions. Industry leaders may be part of the management council	The promoter depends on the agency for all inputs. The agency suffers a risk of incurring loss of time and opportunity if the event fails to exposed to

No	Interpretation grid	Corporate clients	Associations	Sponsor events
		many a problem area in the earlier edition. The client would expect validations at every stage, and this can demotivate the agency team while working on the project. Initial phase of discussions till the point of attaining confidence will be a slippery terrain.	and hence the agency need to be specific and professional in their approach The association will have access to many prominent vendors/ partners; hence price points need to be dealt with transparency.	move forward at any time The agency also suffers a set back if the promoter decides to pull back closer to the date of the event. Closer to the date, the agency may have to take more load as they may realize the issues between sponsors vs. promoter understanding.
3	Strengths that can be leveraged for winning the assignment	Complete and detail-oriented supportive role can win their confidence. Involve key managers from the agency to show them the strength of the agency Offering a one stop solution format will be best suited and will work to the advantage of the agency.	Share concept notes of similar assignments. Appreciation won from the government Bodies will greatly help. Industry references are key to winning the assignment. If the management council is convinced then the agency stands a very high chance of continuous and repetitive business.	This event can be used as a platform to meet new clients If the agency succeeds this can be an entirely new scope of business. Dedicated resource personnel would be needed for this activity which can deprive the agency of using the personnel so allocated for other events that may come up.

No	Interpretation grid	Corporate clients	Associations	Sponsor events
		Designing the event and the product unveiling novelty fused with detailed illustrations and mood board is an opportunity to win the client forever.		
4	Differentiator	Subtle innovations that would impress the invitees. A novel unveiling and a technology fused experience. On time delivery and no deviation on the experience from what has been committed. Involve the client is taking decisions at the initial stages and set targets for deliveries of actions and ensure strict adherence. Time-bound action plans.	Pitch the expo as an experience not to be missed. Involve the members of management council in the deliberations of the event designing and ensure they are convinced about the agency conviction in making the event special and memorable Sensitivity to Protocols.	Innovating sponsor exposure opportunities Identifying new partners for on-line promotion Designing new formats for promotion using print and electronic media. Working close with celebrity performers can give an edge to agency in using the talent to promote and offer superlative experience in the event designing.
5	Market Intelligence	As an established agency it is easy to gather information of the previous edition.	As an established agency it is easy to gather information of the previous edition.	As an established agency it is easy to gather information of the previous edition.

No	Interpretation grid	Corporate clients	Associations	Sponsor events
		Our partners/vendors and the venue where the earlier edition happened are definitely an immediate source of information.	Our partners/vendors and the venue where the earlier edition happened are definitely an immediate source of information.	Our partners/vendors and the venue where the earlier edition happened are definitely an immediate source of information.
		There are other means of gathering intelligence information which are primarily through network and industry contacts.	There are other means of gathering intelligence information which are primarily through network and industry contacts.	There are other means of gathering intelligence information which are primarily through network and industry contacts.
6	Pricing	Though the client has had a bad experience, the estimate they would have will be more or less the same as last time. Most clients fail to realize that enhanced quality and experience does not come cheap. The pricing need to be dynamic and a Building block model need to be adopted.	Detailed pricing sheet sharing all costs is a clear win in this category of events. Justification for spends need to be addressed in detail as the association will audit in detail. Capturing all heads of expenses before signing the contract is important as any additions may not be entertained.	This category is more governed by the quantum of sponsorship a client wills to commit. The quantum of sponsorship committed by the main sponsor decides the number of sponsors that would be required to support the cause. Agency can work on a pricing of either a percentage of the sponsorships generated or a minimum guaranteed pricing plus a sweat payment mode.

No	Interpretation grid	Corporate clients	Associations	Sponsor events
		Working on a thin margin on necessary supports and on better margins on "novelty," "innovation" works in favour of winning contract. Adopting a concept of cost plus agency margin works well.	Keep cost of any special segments separate and inform the members ahead of time.	

e. Factors That Influence Clients While Choosing the Event Design Agency

The following chart provides a graphical representation of the factors that client value while selecting the agency. Each category has their unique requirements and the selection criteria are based on 4 key factors which aid in the decision.

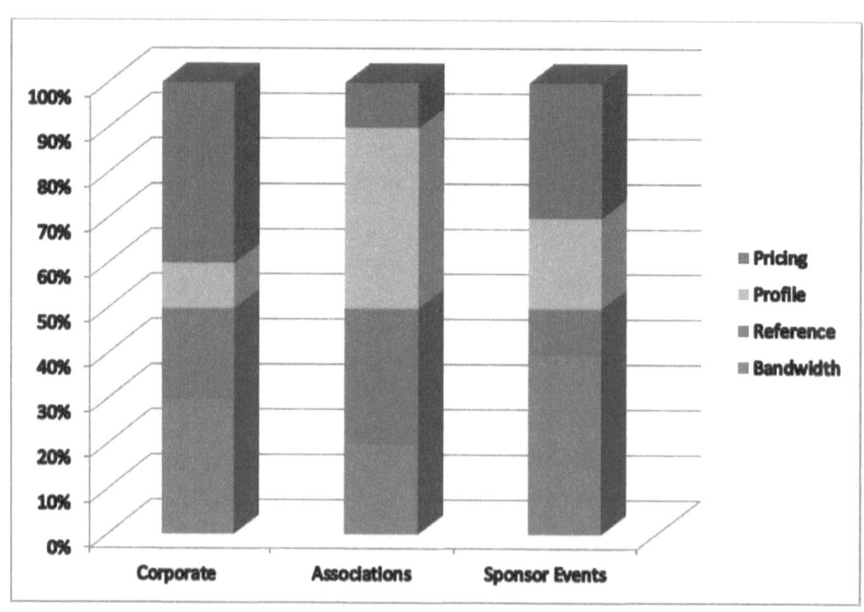

The Art of Building Experiential Events

Bandwidth: This represents the capability of the agency to handle the event providing 360 degree support. The clients in the corporate and sponsorship event category insist on the "bandwidth" and will do industry checks to evaluate and validate the proposal.

Reference: This aspect is the testimonials, or vouching of the capability of the agency. The reference plays a vital role in association and corporate event. The sensitivity of designing an event is very critical in the corporate and association events and hence reference is an important factor.

Profile: The agency profile relates to the size, and the brand value of the agency. Under the category of association and sponsor events, the profile of the event design agency matters as the name of the agency brings in additional value to the portfolio of the promoters. In a corporate event, the event design agency does not get prominence and hence this factor is not of utmost importance.

Pricing: This is a crucial factor across all assignments. The corporate, sponsor event lays high importance to pricing, while the association events select an agency, and the requirements are mapped ahead and the estimates are shared with the agency to deliver their services. Invariably in the association events, the negotiations are done more on the value building front while for corporate and social event, pricing is a key factor in decision-making.

There are other factors like market spread, tax compliances, Innovative solutions and technology adaptability which are also factors that are evaluated.

Never get pleased by the hours you put into your work,
rather be proud of the worth you infused into those hours.

– Deepak Swaminathan

Chapter 7

THE IMPORTANCE OF A VENUE FOR CONDUCTING AN EVENT

While organizing an event, there are many decisions that need to be taken and to arrive at a decision, a combination of challenges, requirements need to be factored. The most important and the first thing to do is "getting a venue."

However, choosing a venue is the one decision that will have the largest impact on your event. Critical planning information, such as the date for the event, is dependent on the venue you select.

It is understandable that the choice of looking for a venue can be challenging and getting one that would suit in all aspects is really tough. Before one embarks on a venue search, the following need to be clear and well-defined.

- The cost allocated for the venue rentals

- The prospective guest count and possible number of attendees

- The event genre: (Awards, Musical, Technical Forum etc.)

Once there is a clear idea of these three things, the search begins. Having the venue booked a minimum of 4–5months in advance will ensure that the date of the event is blocked. This date will logically lead to planning the timeline and milestones that need to be put in place and ensure it works well until the event happens. Additionally, this will give ample time to market the event, if it is an event that would involve the public.

Finding the right venue for your event can be a time-consuming effort. Presented below are some quick action points that would help identify the right venue and availability.

- List down the available convention centres (stand alone and Hotel Banquets) in your city in order of popularity.

- Collect and collate data on the specifications of these venues.

- Get layout and dimensions and discuss with your operations team on the viability of such venues.

- Get a rate quote from the venues shortlisted and get clear inputs on all rules and regulations.

- Leading agencies have a network of venue facilitators who gets the best offer and will also help block the dates that are required.

a. Location, Proximity, Accessibility

A convenient location brings in lots of convenience to the event. Be it the organizer, be it the vendors, be it the guests. With increasing traffic snarls, it is ideal to host an event which is ideally located for guests to quickly reach either from work or home.

It may so happen that the said event might be an expo which means many attendees might be travelling from other towns, hence in such cases it would ideal to host such events which are in the proximity of hotels and airports, rail heads. For residential conferences, it is suggested to host the event in a hotel venue that can offer rooms at different tariffs for the delegates to stay at the event venue, which not only saves cost but also saves time.

Prior to concluding an accessible venue, it is critical to note that the venue is accessible for all kinds of guests, including guests with special needs. This apart, accessibility is also critical for emergency services to reach the spot if the need arises, for vendor/partners to easily ship their materials and workforce on time. For this one needs to understand the profile of guests, category of special guests, VIPs, general invitees etc., and then detail the requirements of parking, valet support, entry points etc.

If the event involves women, it is good to understand if children will also take part and if yes, adequate planning in engaging them in a safe zone also needs to be mapped. Alongside the points mentioned herein, the agency need to work on the safe assembly point, identify the location, plan the routes to reach there, in emergency, spot locations to fabricate necessary signage.

b. Cost, Ambience, Services and Amenities

1. Venue cost

A large part of the event expense can go towards a venue, typically the venue publish tariffs which are negotiable based on the event profile, the guest count and variables that go along with an event. There are select days in a week when the venues might offer special rates which a smart agency capitalizes on. Flexibility on dates can help in getting a rate discount. With modern day apps, it has become a norm to populate an event using social media to gauge the participation also use the media to send out invites.

2. Expense towards ambience at the venue

If the venue is not maintained well, then that adds up to the spend of the agency. While booking a venue, special care need to be taken on the upkeep, the wall panelling, the flooring, entrance doors, backstage, accommodation. A badly maintained venue can be an agency's nightmare as the cost of décor for the venue will escalate and will impact the profitability.

3. Service amenities

In addition to the ambience, it is also important to take into account the service amenities the venue offers; a quick check on the following is advisable:

- Does the venue offer cooking facilities and will it suffice your requirement.
- Do they allow your preferred partner to provide the necessary cooking at the venue?
- What are the do's and don'ts for using the cooking facility?
- The charges for using the cooking facility.
- Does the venue offer housekeeping support or is it to be paid additionally.
- Permissions, licenses that would be required for setting up the kitchen/ cooking facility.
- The designated area for serving the food.
- Has the venue hosted luncheon sessions earlier? If yes, understand the modalities.
- Do they offer furniture support or is it outsourced at a cost? Run a list of furniture you would look for.
- Sound, lights installation at the venue and their usability.
- Do they offer projections, televisions, video camera etc. on hire or are these part of the venue.

c. Minimum Guarantee, Capacity

1. Minimum guarantee

Every venue proposes a rate based on the guarantee of guests who would attend. In short, the space is sold proportionate to the number of seats. An established agency with its wide network can negotiate a flexible guarantee model, where an overflow of upto 10–15% will not be charged for. However if the guarantee falls, then the venue reserves the right to charge for the guaranteed seats and the agency is at loss. Hence it is wise to plan tight and offer a guarantee rather than be sorry later.

2. Capacity

The venue capacity is defined by the type of seating and the space allocation for different activities that are being proposed. The venue charges vary based on application and usage. However depending on the genre of the event, the venue charges vary and is also related to the season and duration of the event. With experience, it is best advised to identify a venue which can accommodate an additional 10% inflow of guests

d. Parking, Layout

1. Parking

Does the venue offer adequate parking for guest vehicles? Do they offer valet parking? A venue with adequate parking space is a desired one. In most venues, they have space arrangements with nearby venues where cars/vehicles can be parked. It is in the interest of the event, that the agency need to discuss these issues with the venue officer to ensure enough parking space is made available. The following have been tried by successful agencies which can lend a ready and well-researched solution.

- If your event is on a weekend, connect with neighbouring offices to request for their parking at a fee.

- Government-owned parks and playgrounds can be an option to evaluate.

- Tie-up with app defined car rental services to pick up and drop guests.

- Vehicle pooling can be an effective alternative.

- Valet parking is a definite requirement.

- Schools and colleges nearby can also be an alternative parking lot with shuttle services.

2. Layout

Even before signing up a venue for an event, it is necessary to evaluate if the venue suits the requirements in all aspects, including meeting the expectations of the potential partners who would work towards the execution of the event.

The Art of Building Experiential Events

Though one will be finding the venue early in the event planning process, it is advisable to get the layout and operations team to draw out the space management clearly mapping the locations vis-à-vis the requirements. This should be the pre-step to confirming the venue. While working on the venue selection, get a detailed floor plan of each venue, and conduct a guided tour of the venue with your teams taking note of points relevant to your event. The layout and floor plan will help in smooth planning and conduct of the event. While drafting and designing the layout, it is advisable to cover the following points.

- Guest reception and registration point
- Venues for each activity and the respective traffic movement between venues
- Locations for placing AV equipment, camera and surveillance teams
- Space for lunch and the capacity it can hold at any given time
- Alighting points for special guests and leadership
- Concurrent event activities and the space required
- Parking for emergency services
- Holding point of event related collaterals and mementoes
- Space for the working teams and their offices
- Security and safety posts
- Clear route to the emergency assembly point.

e. Insurance, Contract Manpower, Acoustics

1. Insurance

Insurance at the face of it might look like an expense that adds up to the cost of an event, but in reality it is a safety net that cannot be compromised. There are many clients who refuse to do business if you are not insured. The new policies of global corporates insist on insuring to cover up liability incurred by infringement of their assets and properties even if it is outside their site. The types of insurance that can be availed are:

- General insurance against event cancellation
- Workmen compensation policy
- Theft, loss for agency as also for client properties
- Calamity insurance

2. Contract manpower

Any event of a reasonable scale that involves over 250 guests will need the support of contract manpower. Contract manpower, are a set of semi-skilled and skilled workforce who are trained in specific areas for the purpose of managing events. This workforce is available at a cost and they represent the agency for a fixed time period as governed by their contract. The following are the areas contract workforce are used

- Registration
- Security and safety operations
- Hostess and runners for an event
- Waiters for the lounge that supports the special invitees
- Back office assistants
- Help desk resources
- Green room managers
- Site support teams

3. Acoustics

If you have experiences loud noise, uneasy audio, blaring sound and poor quality of sound, then the acoustics need to be checked and changed if necessary. Acoustics is just a fancy word for how sound travels through the venue. Acoustic is actually an integral part of the event experience. A high ceiling with low audience capacity can produce a disturbing echo, a low ceiling with improper sound set up can become painfully louder.

Acoustics planning is in itself is a very detailed grid that needs to be developed with customization. The venue size, the ceiling height, the finish of the venue, the kind of seating, the maximum and minimum number of expected attendees, the seating layout etc. are studied along with a separate presenter grid which captures the type of presentation, the contents, the presenter profile etc. are mapped and then merged together to design the ideal acoustic support that would be required.

Planning a delay speaker layout with cloud spots across the event venue with the help of decibel meters and smart deployment of high frequency microphones is another smart way designing effective acoustics.

The above clearly defines that there is a lot to consider when choosing a venue. However, if you take the above into consideration when doing your research, you'll find the perfect venue for your event.

The Art of Building Experiential Events

Frustration & perfection are two dynamically opposite poles, the minute you are able to tame these, there ignites a dynamic enterprise.

– Deepak Swaminathan

Chapter 8

FACTORS THAT ARE CRITICAL IN DESIGNING AN EVENT FOR A CORPORATE

Presenting below is a typical format that is articulated with a client before designing an event. These are designed to set the tone for designing and all Q's are related to the expectations set by the client and would match the overall delivery.

a. Preliminary Client Discussion (Dialogue Interface Document)

Presenting below is a dialogue mapped into an "event understanding" document which has been evolved by the author and has been the primary document in designing an event. The first cut video call was scheduled 3 months prior to the scheduled date of the event.

The first communication exchanged soon after a video call where the agency profile was presented

We are working on the following as per our last discussion. Find below the points that have been mapped further to our discussion, based on which the designing is to be commenced.

1. Identifying venues for Chennai and Mumbai
2. We have captured the requirements as discussed
3. We have presented below the points of responsibilities in a broad spectrum
4. We will revert with venue availability by tomorrow as discussed to take things further

The following points are shared with a client soon after the completion of event briefing

The following are the broad discussions we have had on the event scheduled in Chennai and Mumbai as per details below:

Event Specs:

- The event – A venture fund investment bankers' event.
- Purpose – Evaluate performance of their investments.
- Add on – To evaluate new opportunities for investment.
- This is an evening program from 18:00–22:30 hrs.
- The event is at Chennai/Mumbai on subsequent Fridays.
- The 3rd and 4th week of the last month of 2nd quarter.
- The group size of 40–50 investment bankers and 30 delegates from their invested organizations.
- There would an open presentation followed by breakaway gallery walk session and then network dinner.
- Entertainment to be discussed and proposed further.
- The properties to be 5 star with good banquet facility to hold the conference as also a display gallery.
- There could be a requirement for a separate discussion room (typically like a business lounge on standby).
- There could be room requirements, which we will communicate shortly to the hotel.

The following actions were to be done by the agency and shared to client by 6th May

- Identifying and proposing venues across chennai and mumbai – last week of the 1st quarter
- List of preferred hotels were shared with the client and preferences obtained
- Venue required for set up from the previous midnight of the show
- Gallery display space (preferably another room)
- Business lounge as stand by
- Cluster seating with stage
- Dais to accommodate LED or projectors
- Buffet dinner with cocktail to be planned
- Also evaluate if dinner can be served at the lawns, as a choice (though it is rainy season in mumbai then)

Responsibility of the event agency:

- Venue identification
- Designing of all event collaterals
- Coordinate with portfolio firms to set up booth
- Standardizing booth design
- Follow up with portfolio companies on the do's and don'ts
- Registration at site
- Sound, lights, projection support for the event
- Entertainment options to be discussed and concluded
- Folders designing, development and printing for the participating firms
- Professional master of ceremonies
- Hotel facilitation
- Video presentation/slides/spec cards as per CIP

Responsibility of the client:

- Mail appointing the agency as event designers to negotiate with venues
- Brand logo and colour schemes to be shared with media point
- Agenda and event flow to be proposed
- Validation of concept notes and costs
- In principle cost approvals towards the hotel costs, event execution cost

b. List of Points That Would Elicit the Objective (Sample List of Questionnaire)

Client response are in **BOLD**

- Dates proposed for the events at Mumbai and Chennai – **End of 3rd quarter.**
- Number of guests at each location – **Around 40 to 50 from the investment banker team + 30 delegates.**
- Preference of the hotel category at the 2 cities – **5 star hotels (Prefer rooms to be at the same venue).**
- Are any rooms required for invitees – **20 rooms.**
- Duration of the event (business Session + Network time) – **3 to 4 hours.**

- Profile of guests/invitees/expats and nationals – **HNI, institutional investors, majority Indian, some foreigners.**

- Is there any "inaugural" gig planned – **No.**

- Is projection/live streaming required – **Yes.**

- Technology interface requirement (voting pads, event app, short film on the brands invested in) – **Yes.**

- Video call facility – **Yes, to connect guests from Middle East.**

- Testimonials for display – **Yes.**

- Head table/chair, Co-chair – **No.**

- Is a moderator guided session planned – **Not as of now. We have not considered running the format in this manner not to say we will not consider it.**

- MC/Host for the event – **Yes.**

- Branded stationery kits specific to the business session – **Yes.**

- Delegate kit – **We may want to have a book with the updates for investors.**

- Theme for the event – **Investment conclave.**

- Take away gifts – **Yes each of the portfolio companies will have stall where people can check details/products on the company and potentially take away gifts.**

- Thought leader speech session (if this is required, we can recommend) – **No.**

- Event memorabilia – **No.**

- Unveiling of the event (TBD) – **We will revert on the same.**

- F&B preferences – **Buffet and drinks to be included.**

- Designing support – **Yes.**

- PR agency appointment and management – **No.**

- Registration/RSVP support – **Yes.**

- Entertainment briefing (genre)–musical – **Regional/Classical.**

- Local Logistic support in each city – **Yes.**

- Photography (instant exposure as a Take away) – **Yes.**

- Videography (including live bytes and online edits) – **Yes.**

- Sound, lights, power for the event – **Yes.**

- Any other inputs – **All our expectations have been covered.**

The Art of Building Experiential Events

c. Venue Recce, Identifying the Right Location for an Event – the Actions Taken by the Agency Logistic Coordination Team Is Presented in a Table Format

The points to note when you have a multicity/multi-country road show and working with venue partners:

- When the client is requesting for a star category venue, it is ideal to look for a brand which is present across the cities/country where you are proposing the event.

- When negotiating the deal for multi-location, the agency can negotiate an attractive pricing for the client.

- It is also encouraged to negotiate few rooms as a value-add for the agency team, with the concurrence of the client, which is always a welcome.

- Working on a special menu, local delights, customization comes as goodwill if partnered with the same venue brand.

- Benefits like free Wi-Fi, complimentary use of business centre and free lounge access for the leadership of the client are possible when partnered with the same brand across cities/countries.

No	Points covered with the venue partner	Brand 1	Brand 2	Brand 3
1	Location and accessibility of the venue from the airport	CBD; 20 km	Downtown; 10 km	Outside city; 40 km
2	Dimension of the Main Event venue	300 sqmtr	250 sqmtr	250 sqmtr
3	Space for the gallery display	400 sqmtr	300 sqmtr	275 sqmtr
4	Lead time for set up without load	12 hours (comp)	6 hours; beyond 6 hours will be chargeable	Every hour of set up if chargeable
5	Seating style and linen décor	Cluster with choice of colours	Cluster with choice of colours	2 choices available

No	Points covered with the venue partner	Brand 1	Brand 2	Brand 3
6	Ambience of the venue	Stylish	Sober	Due for change
7	Parking facility and valet support	Limited parking with Valet support	Parking with limited valet support	Lots of parking space
8	F&B rate	USD 50 p.pax	USD 38 p.pax	USD 45 p.pax
9	Hall Rentals	Nil (provided we commit both road show with minimum guarantee of 75 pax)	USD 200 per additional hour beyond 6 hours	USD 300 per hour
10	Value adds	Free Wi-Fi Complimentary room upgrade for leadership Live counters	Free Wi-Fi Comp room for agency	Free Wi-Fi Free Lounge access
11	Room category and Tariff	USD 80 per night	USD 70 per night	USD 100 per night
12	Is any license required for performances	Yes, if you have an International Music band	No	No
13	Payment terms and credit	Advance of 50% Balance with a Banker signed contract	100% Advance	75% Advance 25% on day of show
14	Cocktail Rates	On Actual as per published tariff card	USD 30 p.pax	USD 25 p.pax
15	Mock demo completion of the set up	Validated by agency	Can organize upon signing up	Photographs of earlier set up shared
16	Venue snaps	Shared	Shared	Shared

With the above inputs the agency and client evaluate merits and demerits of each venue and signs up the suitable partner.

d. Preparation of The "Design Document" (Thoughts, Flow and Choices)

Presented below is a sample document prepared by the author in designing an event. The document is a real time event, which was designed and executed for a leading brand from the category of home coats.

Client: Leading brand of Paints for Business and Residences

Event: Dealer Meet and Product Launch

Event Date and Time –mm/yy (Day)18:00 hrs.– 22:00 hrs.

Venue: Leading Hotel Banquets

AgencyDocument: v1/mm.dd.yy

Premise

Paints, a formidable organization in the business of coatings has grown from a medium sized south focussed company to being a national player. The growth has been consistent with increase in presence and in the variety of Innovative Products unveiled.

Event objective

Aligned to the growth strategy, Paints is set to unveil 3 novel paints at an exclusive dealer meet proposed in mm/yy. The invitees being the "dealer partners" from across India, the expectations and the experience need to match the brand persona and also the vision of the organization. In an otherwise crowded market space, the brand has carved a niche for itself unveiling "new age concepts" in paints that has won the appreciation and recognition of the "green council" which has given an edge over competition.

The event outline

- Core objective moderation session
- Interactive game on the brand and its USPs
- A flash on the new facility that has been inaugurated recently
- A corporate AV
- Special bytes with "strategic communication" and "key messages"

- Interactive segments with local flavour entertainment
- Innovation for scheme unveiling (optional)

The experience thought

- To design an experience that would create an "awe" for the new products to be unveiled
- Present the brand as a formidable player and a brand "to be with"
- Build a sense of warmth for the dealers by creating exclusive interactive segments
- Present a holistic view of the "journey and the vision ahead"
- Build a launch experience that will fuse well in "style and substance" to the new products
- Power packed evening with the best mix of "corporate" "brand" "products" "experience" "entertainment"
- Special element of "thought leadership" can be discussed as an option
- Platform for exchange of views, success stories, challenges and "way forward" discussions will form part of the event experience.

Event flow

- Welcome surprise
- Thought leadership session/moderation session
- Interactive game with guests and a product based "view point" game
- Unveiling experience and post unveiling views
- Key address and facilitations
- Entertainment
- Thanks and take away

Event choices

No	Launch – "thought" – based on choice the costs will be proposed to the client	Reference snap
1	**Step no-churn –** A proprietary of the agency. This is the latest trend in unveiling new products among stakeholders, dealers and partners. An interactive gig with specialized performers in live with virtual wall interaction. The storyboard is developed with the "core" messages and the dancers interact with synced movements between the virtual wall and live performances. The product in unveiled in a musical story format and concludes with live "product" walk on the dais.	
2	**Graphic shot and 3D animation** An android is used for the unveiling and the end of a dance sequence and the selected guest energizes the Android tablet and the sequence of unveiling happens on the LED wall. Well knitted graphics woven with the story of the new products in weaved together to form the core for the unveiling. A 3 minute graphic and 3D Animation leads to the virtual product and followed by the live "product" walk on the dais.	

No	Launch – "thought" – based on choice the costs will be proposed to the client	Reference snap
3	Traditional Unveiling Tried and tested format of sliding panels that unveils the 3 products simultaneously with special lighting and specially edited launch BGM. The dealers would have experienced this earlier and may not find this in absolute "awe," nevertheless this is a format that is being practised by many event teams. The product is unveiled when the sliding panels open with the dummy cut outs are visible	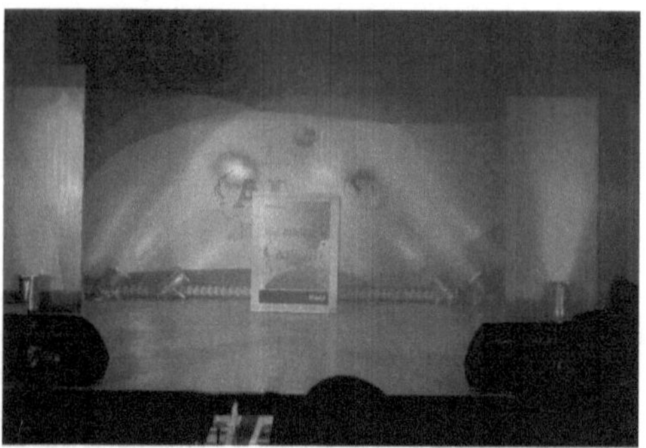
4	Thematic Fashion Walk leading to unveiling A story based Fashion walk that captures the "Vision" and "Mission" of the Brand and its Journey. The story evolves from the time of a single product to a stature of "Varieties for Choice" today and relevant USP's are fused into the gig which culminates with the New Product Unveiling and the new products are showcased. The product also kept on a display post launch.	

The above document is a sample of the event thought and design which the agency presents to the client with ideal solutions that would suit their Brand Persona. The options are proposed aligned to the guests, the objective, and the purpose of the event. Once the right choices are proposed, the client and agency engage with the communication team, to work on fine tuning the event.

e. Event Flow With Specific "Check Points" (Sample List)

The chart details the date wise actions that need to be done prior to an event with responsibility. This chart is shared internally and the production head and the project head are key supervisors to ensure nil deviation. The chart is a ready checklist with the responsibility clearly defined among the stakeholders.

Event: Annual Conference Venue: XXXX

No	Jobs to be done	Agency resp	Client approval
1	**Designs for the event**	Sam	Joe
	1. Backdrop for the day conference		
	2. Awards Nite backdrop		
	3. Standees		
	4. Board at the Entrance of the hotel		
	5. Pile on in the drive way of the property		
	6. Theme prop in the event banquet		
2	**Other designs as required by the client**	Anto	Leyan
	1. Delegate Coach Sticker – size 9" * 12"		
	2. Banners for Bus station – 3ft * 5ft		
	3. Placard for the airport – 3ft * 2ft		
	4. Cover for Gift Coupon – size 1/3 of A4		
	5. Gift voucher – collect from Sandy and organize		
	6. Certificate – Names to be added and a new category to be added		
	7. Tent Cards in Room – 9" * 6"		
	8. Agenda sheet with just branding		

No	Jobs to be done	Agency resp	Client approval
	9. Design for the cake to be handed over to the hotel		
	10. Conference Presentation Template		
	11. Badges – design to be done and sent for production		
	12. Invitation for Dinner with Leadership		
3	**Events that we need to execute:**	Andy	Joe
	1. 5th April – Day conference – 140 pax in theatre and 12 pax Cluster		
	2. 5th April post lunch session – 150 pax in theatre and 12 pax Cluster		
	3. 6th April – Day conference – 225 pax – all in theatre style		
	4. 6th April Awards Nite – 220 pax in theatre and 10 pax in Sofas		
4	**Prop details**	Andy	Jai
	Fabrication – Day 1		
	Standee in Venue 6'/3' X 6 Nos	108 sqft	
	Welcome Board Hotel Entrance 8/8' X 1 No	64 Sqft	
	Set up – Day 2		
	Stage Blue Carpet and Steps 24'/16'/1.5'	384 Sqft	
	Backdrop 24'/8' X 1 No	192 Sqft	
	Side Wings 8'/3' X 2 Nos	48 Sqft	
	AV Masking 10'/9.5' X 2 Nos	190 Sqft	
	Standee 6'/3' X 4 Nos	72 Sqft	
	Welcome Standee 6'/3' X 2 Nos	36 sqft	
		1094 Sqft	
	Gala Evening		
	Same Backdrop New Flex	1 no	
	Same Side Wings New Flex	2 no	
	Goal Post Truss for lights 26'/12' X 1 No	64 Ft	
5	**sound, Light support that we need to provide**		

No	Jobs to be done	Agency resp	Client approval
	1. Day 1 – Sound and lights for 150 pax with 2 projectors and Photography		
	2. Day 2 – Sound and lights for 225 pax with 2 projectors, photo and video		
	3. Gala Evening – enhanced sound, lights, projectors, photo and video		
6	**What you will carry from base**	Karan	
	1. The White non-slippery mats for the dais to be used on Day 2		
	2. The Print materials for all standees and support props		
7	**Entertainment for the awards nite**	Anto	Joe
	1. Dual Band – Lady Minus Track Band		
	2. DJ		
	3. Stand-up comedy – Subhir Khan		
	4. Choreography – 6/8 members team		
8	**Bouquets requirement**	Sam	Jai
	1. Day 1 @ 09:00 hrs. – 5 Nos		
	2. Day 2 @ 10:00 hrs. – 5 nos for the day		
9	**Contact at the property**		
	Head of Sales – +9188540247122		
10	**Generator support provided by us**	Anto	Joe
	1. Day 1 – Power required to be given by hotel		
	2. Day 2 – Generator being brought in by us		
11	**License – all organized by the hotel and paid by the client directly**	Agency	Client to approve

f. Final Execution Document with Detailing of Designs (3D Layouts, 2D Layouts and Seating Plan for Optimum Guest Experience)

Presented below is a sample document that is part of the event execution department that captures all the essential elements that need to be planned and incorporated for effective management

Event Design and Management Checklist

No	Item head
1	Distance from Airport to the Venue.
2	Distance from Rail head and time to reach the venue.
3	Exact Address and Landmark for guests to reach the venue.
4	Pickup plan from Airport for Top Management.
5	Check-intimeat the property – 12:00 hrs.
6	Checkout on late checkout.
7	Additional room for break out Conference for 30 pax on Day 1
8	Conference for 250 pax on Day 1
9	Theme logo Cake – Day 1 @ 15:00 hrs.
10	Open air lawns for evening function – Clusters.
11	Is License required for evening function? If yes advice cost details.
12	How much power can you provide?
13	How many rooms in the property and category of rooms facilities in room.
14	Quick check-in for special guests.
15	Welcome Drink on arrival.
16	What welcome surprise can you give for guests?
17	Special courtesies on arrival.
18	Enough Bell desk to support luggage transfers.
19	If there are 2 properties then distance between them.
20	What is the transport arrangement between the two properties?
21	Daily transfers, how do you propose to do?
22	What about Bed/tea for guests at the 2 hotels.
23	Branding of Morning papers.
24	Do you have local cable channels to put our message?
25	Do the other properties have Gym and Pool?
26	What leisure activity is possible in the Evenings post conference?
27	Do you have a hotel band to entertain the guests?
28	Which are the restaurants they would have B/f, Lunch and Dinner?
29	Is the breakfast served in respective Hotels?
30	What permissions are required for the sightseeing?
31	We need to transport 240 pax for sightseeing, plan logistics.
32	Can we have 2 morning sessions of Yoga training for guests?
33	Room brandings would happen and u need to help us do it.

The Art of Building Experiential Events

No	Item head
34	We would have surprise gifts for guests which needs to be placed in the room.
35	What is the size of the lawns proposed for the evening function?
36	Which is a special local flavoured Desert that can be provided?
37	What ethnic local cuisine that you can serve for the gala dinner?
38	Bonfire required on the arriving evening.
39	A separate Lounge for breakfast for 30 pax required for Day 2
40	We would brand with a welcome message at lobby, food court etc.
41	A Who-is-in-which-room list is a must on all rooms.
42	Emergency number in all rooms a must.
43	A doctor on call necessary.
44	Do you have a travel desk ready?
45	Liquor Choice and pricing? And Cocktail snack rate?
46	Bill to company for balance payments and F&B costs.
47	You need to check phones, hot water facilities,etc. in all rooms.
48	Fumigation a must for open air.
49	What is the normal temperature during the proposed time of the year?
50	Need exact dimensions of the hall allocated.
51	Seating for Day 1 is board room style and for Day 2 is Class Room.
52	Hotel to brief client team on safe assembly and emergency evacuation plans.
53	Special Upgrade for the MD and Board Members.
54	What sport activities can be offered.
55	The best sightseeing places and their distances and your rates.
56	How much time do we allocate for sightseeing?
57	Can we have professional guides for the sightseeing?
58	Safety medicines and turn-around time on request.
59	Branding of vehicles and numbers.
60	Room for storing event props.
61	Do you have staff canteen for event workforce.
62	Fireworks may be required on the awards nite–Are Any licenses required.
63	We would erect a dais in the indoor for the conference.
64	Seating on the dais will be 6–7 pax; need artistic wooden chairs.
65	F&B support for the indoor conference and location of buffet.
66	Sound, lights and projectors will be provided by the agency.
67	Locate spot to place the genset.

No	Item head
68	UPS support and technician mandatory for all events.
69	Large décor dais for the outdoor event.
70	Cocktail at the outdoor.
71	DJ will play till midnight on the awards nite.

Props Details

No	Description branding	Ht	Sizes Width	Units	Location @ Site
1	Arch Pillar (box type)	12 ft	3 ft	2 – (4 sides)	Main Gate
	Arch top	24 ft	3 ft	1 – (4 sides)	
	Arch top sides	24 ft	1 ft	2	
2	Route Boards (external)	6 ft	3ft	10	Critical points
	Direction boards – Parking, Food Lounge, Event Wash Rooms, Display Zone (each 2 panels)	8 ft	3 ft	10	At strategic points on site
3	Welcome near Admin building	10 ft	10 ft	1	Admin Building entrance
4	Welcome Board	8 ft	3 ft	2	At reception point
5	Pile on-internal Map " you are here"	10 ft	4 ft	2	Reception and pre-event area
6	Show and Tell 4 Booths – Centre panel	10 ft	10 ft	4	Pre-event lounge
	Show and Tell Booth – side Panels	10 ft	6 ft	8	Pre-event lounge
7	Legacy Standees	8 ft	3 ft	8	Pre-event lounge

No	Description		Sizes	Units	Location @ Site
	branding	Ht	Width		
8	STAGE COMPONENTS				
	Backdrop	12 ft	40 ft	1	At event area
	Side wings	12 ft	4 ft	2	
	AV Masking (LED Wall size 8 ftht x 10 ft)	14.5 ft	14 ft	2	
	Stage Skirting	2.5 ft	40 ft	1	
	Stage Skirting sides	2.5 ft	10 ft	2	
	plaque design for granite stone	3 ft	4 ft	1	At Reception
	side wall design (encompassing 4 sides)	8 ft	20 ft	1	Periphery for event venue
	Podium	4 ft	2 ft	3	
9	Sapling name card design (brass plate)	.5 ft	1 ft	4	

The above documents contain information with regard to the brand collaterals, the placements and the sizes which are matched with the design teams. Once the props are ready for dispatch, the operation team numbers them in a combination of alpha numeric grid and the same is dispatched with a delivery note to the site.

The site operation team receives the same and cross checks the prints before erecting them. The props so received at site, is also rechecked for quality of production and if any damages are found, the same is corrected before erecting those.

The master sheet of responsibility is the most important document that needs to be carefully prepared, the list of props, the placements, the design perspective, the acoustics, the layout of seats, the segregation of guests between VVIPS's and others, are all mapped in the master document.

A time wise action plan grid is also prepared to ensure clockwork precision and handling of event. The entire team at the agency spends considerable time planning for a seamless execution of the event. All department heads are debriefed on the client expectations, the critical requirements, and minute check points among other routine points.

The event document also features the exact location of the prop which is shared as a e-document with reference photograph as appended below.

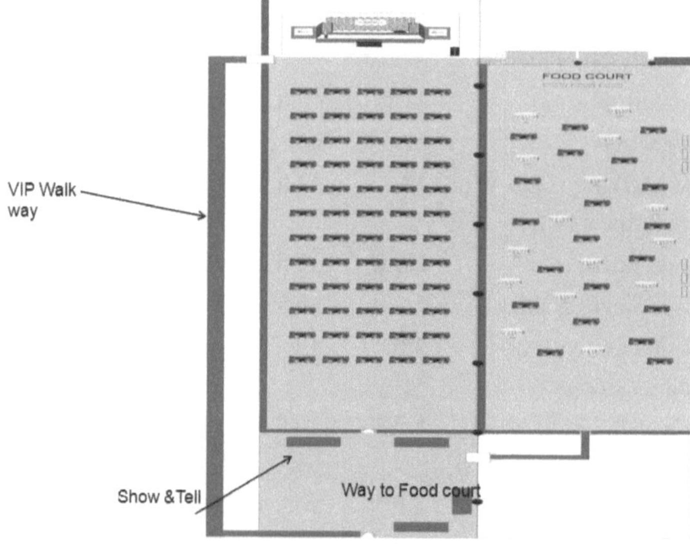

The close up perspective of the dais is also shared with the client for their validations and the approved design is sent for production and erection.

Unveiling Perception shared with the client

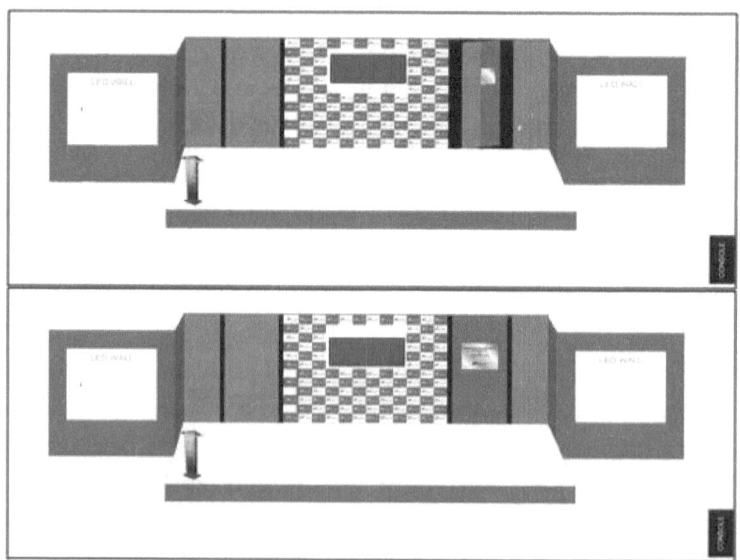

The Art of Building Experiential Events

g. Guest Interface and "WOW" Elements

It is the duty of the event design agency to plant subtle yet memorable surprises in an event. The surprises, so designed are proposed based on the profile of the audience, the persona of the Corporate and the brand statement.

The WOW element intervention (ambience and support)

Lighting	Sound
Ambient lighting using special efx illumination in sync with the brand colors and product colors, automated pre-programmed lighting systems to match the mood of celebration	High End sound systems using delay with optimum sound management that would be apt for the outdoor program, with intelligently panned sound installations
Stage/Dais	**Projection**
Spacious stage with brand panels illuminated and finished with detailing, providing slots for excellent Brand Visibility, adhered to strict safety norms and hues matching the brand colors with safety pointers	Latest technology projection that enables multi-feed capability offering panoramic view as also split views with online concurrent video management
Branding	**Linear Editing**
Theme panels, planned in accordance to retention and Brand Mapping, positioned at vantage points with focus on connecting the brand with our TG	Using drone and multi-camera synced to online editing to capture special moments, as also to capture candid shots to make the event memorable and special

Unveiling and stage perspective

Matrix Laser with Interactivity

The brand is a technology brand, and we proposed use of the latest Human LASER for the unveiling. The use of the laser ushered a new experience

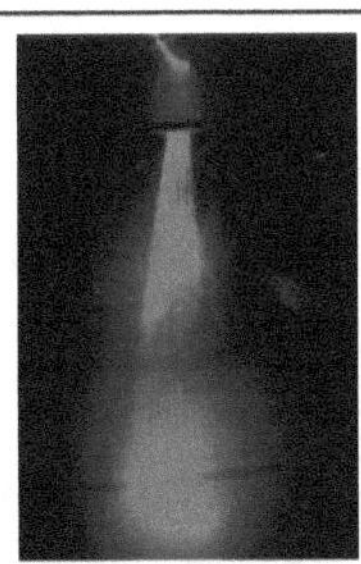

and the unveiling was truly special. The launch had an element of involving the guests who synced to the thumping music and dancing lasers which was well etched in the minds of the guests.

Stage Perception

The client brief was mapped, and the stage décor was planned. The highlight would be a wireless experience and a dash of wide space on the dais which gives a feel of the expanse and makes the set up look grand and colourful. The stage design is shared with 2 views after encompassing all the requirements proposed by the client. This detail presentation helps in minimising last minute rush to complete the unexpected.

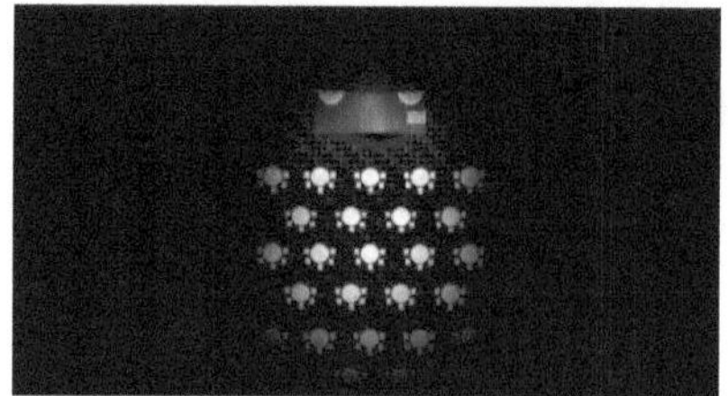

The above are the typical presentations shared with the client on the set perspective, and the WOW elements that are built in. The above are real time samples of events designed and executed by the author through his agency.

h. Plan for Contingencies

It is indeed an irony that this business category is called "EVENT." True to the name the experience can me memorable for 2 reasons, either the EVENT was well appreciated and went without any glitch or the EVENT went the other way filled with learning and challenges right through.

In spite of the best plans, the best teams, efficient execution, there can be multiple issues which can cause an event to derail. The failure of an event is

The Art of Building Experiential Events

invariably attached to the design and execution agency. To overcome the challenges, the agency designs a grid of possible contingencies and adequately briefs the client as also gears up internally to face, manage any contingency.

Shared below is the sample contingency grid developed by the author.

No	Contingency	Preparedness
1	Power Outage	Empanel a vendor with strict guidelines and sign a non-deviation policy
		Vendor to have a standby genset with all cables laid
		Full-fledged team of technicians and stand by electrician to address issues
		Critical areas like basic sound, lights and projectors to be routed via UPS
		Always plan 20% over load as a factor while arriving the power requirement
2	Head Table Seating	Plan the dais to accommodate 2 additional persons than prescribed by client
		Ensure width of stage is designed to accommodate an additional row
		Keep 30% more quantity of head table chairs as a back-up
		Sturdiness of dais to be checked for full house capacity
		Plan additional blank name cards for last minute changes
3	Sound System	May be caused by people tripping over wires, faulty equipment, faulty electrical connections, missing components.
		Contingency plans:
		• Have a back-up sound system
		• Include people with skills to fix such equipment from the Event Management team

No	Contingency	Preparedness
4	Missing staff at the required time	Have a person designated in the Event Management team as a "Troubleshooter" whose job is to continually move about the venue looking for such problems. Roster more staff than are actually needed so that there are a few "spares" that can be assigned to positions anywhere.
5	Floral bunches/ bouquet	Clients often forget this requirement and this many a time springs up as a surprise. It is important to cushion your estimate that includes welcome accessories like a bouquet/floral bunches. The numbers to match the Guest of Honours
6	Mic Runners	Q&A is part of most events and is a definite in dealer meets and symposiums Plan adequate Mic Runners for events Plan 1 runner for every 25 guests for effective turn-around time Brief them on the way the microphone need to be handled Control the microphone from the console to avoid frequency screeches
7	Damages and Loss	Breakages and losses could include High value event props, electrical equipment and lighting, trophies, event paperwork, canteen equipment and supplies, keys, money and many other items. Contingency plans: • Keep spares and back-up systems • Roster on a "trouble shooter" who detect these problems and reports • Roster on other surplus staff whose job it is to contact supplies, run out to stores and/or move about the venue to find items

No	Contingency	Preparedness
8	Injuries and Accidents	• Organize first aid and/or other qualified medical personnel to be in attendance throughout the event • Roster on more staff than the minimum required so that if one person requires treatment it will not impact on the running of the event • Ensure driveways and entrances are not blocked to emergency personnel • Train all event staff what to do in an emergency and when unexpected occur
9	Weather	Particularly affects outdoor events. • In the event of a sudden downpour ensure there is adequate shelter for all else people will start going home and won't come back even if the skies clear • Make plans to relocate activities to sheltered areas or to alter the event programme to salvage the day if possible • Have contingency insurance for your event if there is much at stake financially

i. D-Day Execution and Back-Up Plans

The D-Day of the event and the pre-day of the event are 2 crucial days that decides the fate of the event. Irrespective of the foregone fact that things can go wrong, it is possible to map all the requirements and detail on the discussion table to ensure the team are able to control a broad part of the flow.

Presented below is a chart that typically represents this flow. (Reference grid)

EXPO mm/yy – Work/Responsibility Chart

No	Activity	Responsibility	Status	Back-up
1	Permissions from Venue Office to move stocks inside	Agency	**Completed**	Recommendation contact kept on standby
2	Letter to venue Admin office for detailing manpower at site	Client	**Completed**	Back-up confirmation mail kept ready
3	Designs for the stall	Agency	**Completed**	Alternate design kept as a back-up
4	Approval of designs	Client	**Completed**	Approved and taken a signed copy, CC Chairman
5	Printing of Props	Agency	**Completed**	One new printer kept on standby 24/7
6	Fabrication of the stall as per layout	Agency	**Completed**	Approved and taken a signed copy, CC Chairman
7	Plasma at stall	Agency	**Pending**	3 samples organized for approvals
8	Promoters Finalization	Agency	**Completed**	1 spare added for contingency
9	Badges Designs	Agency	**Completed**	Approved and taken a signed copy, CC Chairman
10	Stall Reader designs	Client	**Completed**	Validated and 1 spare added for contingency
11	Printing of Stall Readers	Agency	**Completed**	Site check pending, technician on standby
12	Printing of Badges	Agency	**Completed**	Approved and taken a signed copy, CC Chairman
13	Printing of Stall Vinyl	Agency	**Completed**	Delivered and quality checked

No	Activity	Responsibility		Status	Back-up
14	Press Release Drafts		Client	**Completed**	Delivered and quality checked
15	Issuing of Press Release	Agency		**Completed**	Client head facilitation to be done at site
16	Gifts for the Event [Take away]	Agency		**Couriered**	Delivered and quality checked
17	Bar stools at stall	Agency		**Pending**	Samples organized for approvals
18	Surprise Gifts for special guests	Agency		**Pending**	Client has cancelled this requirement, but source located at site and kept ready for a last minute change
19	Illusionist Finalization and Booking	Agency		**Completed**	Validated and closed
20	Illusionist Acts * Static Energy theme * Power of Concentration * Remote Mind Power Theme	Agency		**Completed**	Validated and closed
21	Card reader at the stall	Agency		**Completed**	Site check pending, technician on standby
22	Questionnaire for data capture		Client	**Pending**	Approved and taken a signed copy, CC Chairman
23	Briefing of Promoters		Client	**Pending**	Reporting time advanced including spare
24	Reimbursement of Statutory Payments from organizer		Client	**Pending**	Facilitation completed and nominee appointed
25	Coffee Vending machine Hire	Agency		**Pending**	Options kept open for client to decide

No	Activity	Responsibility		Status	Back-up
26	Press guests Invitations	Agency		**Completed**	Approved and taken a signed copy, CC Chairman
27	Briefing of Press guests [16th and 17th]		Client	**Pending**	At site – responsibility client coordinator
28	Interactions with Potential Delegates		Client	**Pending**	At site – responsibility client coordinator
29	Activity Flow of guests	Agency	Client	**Completed**	Discussed and reroute alternative done
30	Scheduling of slots for Illusionists	Agency		**Completed**	Discussed and written document shared
31	Attire for Promoters	Agency		**Completed**	Discussed and written document shared
32	Floral décor at Stall	Agency		**Pending**	Options kept open for client to decide
33	Content for the Plasma		Client	**Completed**	Concluded and new designs on standby
34	Poster for the Illusion show	Agency		**Pending**	Pending for validation
35	Lighting for the stall			**Completed**	Closed
36	Sound for the stall and Lapel Mics			**Pending**	Pending for validation
37	Spec sheets for the guests		Client	**Pending**	Discussed and written document shared
38	Note Pads, Pens, Pen Drive		Client	**Completed**	Delivered and quality checked
39	Shipping of Item 38 [On Request]	Agency		**Pending**	Client is shipping the same
40	Visitor Book at the stall	Agency		**Completed**	Delivered and quality checked

j. Feedback Mechanism

Feedback from the client is valuable and for a service provider it is equivalent to getting paid to learn. The feedback helps not only in correcting the course, but also helps in setting new benchmarks and implementing evaluation pointers that would help in improving the overall experience. Presented below is the fact sheet of feedback.

No	Experiences	Observations (client Inputs)			
1	The designing of the collaterals				
2	The run up planning to the D-Day				
3	Quality of Sound, lights, Projection, and Hosts				
4	Technology interface (experience of using our app)				
5	The floral décor/ protocol management				
6	Product Unveiling experience				
7	Photo, Video quality and delivery				
8	Please Rate us on a scale of 1–10 for the following	Pointers	1–3 (Poor)	4-(Average)	6–7 (Good)	8–10 (Excellent)
		Client service				
		Site operations				
		Project Team				
		Event Directors				
		Design capability				
9	Voice of Pride	Client to share a written or video feedback on their experience of working with the agency			

If our team is our asset, our process our strength, our credibility our pride, what follows is a steady stream of business opportunities.

– Deepak Swaminathan

Chapter 9
DESIGNING A "FACILITY UNVEILING"

a. Key Thought Process behind the Plan

Facility unveiling is a landmark event for an organization. These events are very special events for the organization, and the client would extend all possible support to the selected agency in designing and delivering a World Class Experience.

The facility inauguration acts as a "branding" opportunity too, apart from interactions with the press, getting Government support etc. The facility inauguration is not an annual affair but a very special milestone in the History of any Corporate.

b. Preliminary Client Discussion (Dialogue Interface Document)

To design a facility inauguration, the agency should insist on a preliminary fact finding meet with the decision makers to understand the fibre of the event and their expectations. The discussion would cover the following

- The Date and time of the event

- Detail of the new facility like capacity, size, facilities etc.

- Are there any special recognitions like the "Green Certification" for the facility

- The USP of the facility

- The products that would be rolled out from this facility

- Is this the first unit of the Corporate or otherwise

- If it is an evening function, then is the corporate planning a cocktail dinner?

- Specific directions if any on their preferred Unveiling style.

- Any special Don'ts and Do's from the Corporate.

- Their Corporate Identity Manual.

- Corporate branding docket.

- Logistics for the guests on the D-Day.

- Number of people who would be employed

- Details of technology in force and the Patented technology details if any

- How many guests are likely to be invited

- Profile and break-up of the guests to be invited

- The tentative event flow that the client is discussing

- Does the client plan to invite Government heads/Heads of State etc.

- Protocol details of Government Visitors

- Any specific seating style to be adhered to

- Safety and security mapping

- F&B Partner and plan for locating the kitchen space

- Will there be a requirement to plan a display lounge

- Are there any demos of technology planned, if so details

- Are there any business sessions planned prior or post the event, and the support expected of the agency

- Logistics for the leadership team and their alighting point at the venue

- Permissions from the local authorities.

- Venue entry and exit plans for the visitors and dignitaries.

- Special activities like Plant Sapling, lamp lighting, plaque unveiling.

- Entertainment at welcome point and at the inauguration.

- Power, and all event execution related issues.

- Corporate AV of the client.

- 3D walkthrough of the facility if available.

- Would the event design agency also be involved in designing the event collaterals?

- Entertainment for the opening act on the Dais.

- Is a tour of the facility planned if so, the expectation from the event design agency.

- Designated space for parking with demarcation.

- Entry and exit, safe assembly and safety demo for guests.

The above are the broad points that would emerge from the first meeting basis which the agency team puts up a comprehensive scope document detailing the

The Art of Building Experiential Events

points that have been discussed. The flow of the initial discussions leading up to preparing the event documents can be illustrated as follows

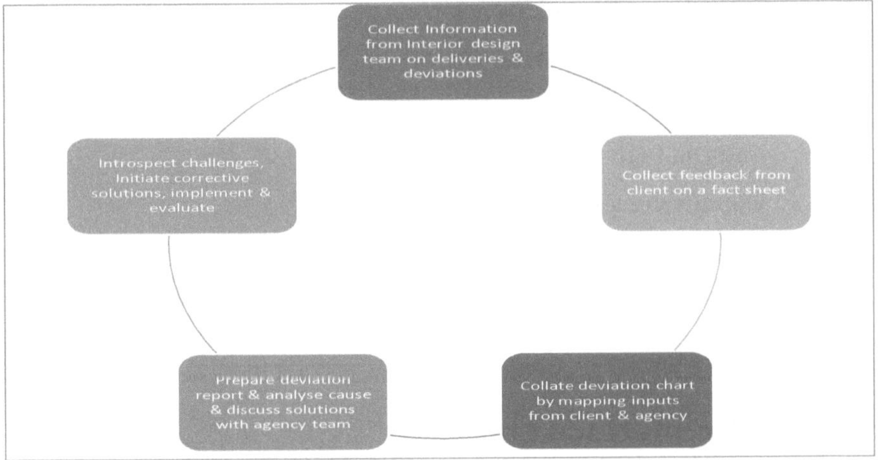

c. Inspection of the Venue

The venue proposed by the client while discussing with the agency may still be under construction and the event design agency will need to work closely with the Interior design team to hasten up the venue and make it event ready by the D-Day.

Presented below is a sample of the event venue which was a facility inauguration assignment handed to the author's agency. The Reece to the venue is a wonderful opportunity for the agency to creatively visualize the event and present a complete sketch fusing all factors. The success of the event design agency lies in the ability to present a visual sketch of the way the agency conceives to the client.

The venue for the inauguration was the site, and when the operation team visited, it was still far from completion. The complexities involved were very high and with just about 6 weeks available for the inauguration, the role of the event agency was demanding and the activity commenced with setting up a site office alongside the Interior design agency to map requirements, propose changes, support at areas that fell short. This exercise tested the capability of the event agency in

A View of the site as it was 6 weeks prior to the event

turning around an incomplete space to an event friendly venue. Few points that were quickly put in place are shared herewith

- Flooring and walls at the venue

- Air con arrangements

- Entry and exit

- Optimum usage of space to have a hold on costs

- F&B Lounge and kitchen area

- Safety and Security plan

Action flow interface chart

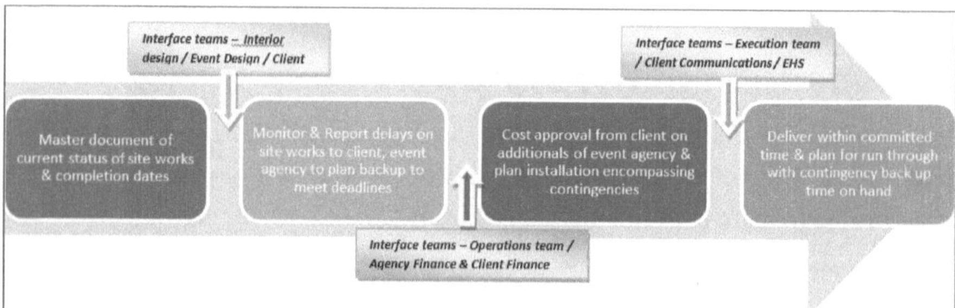

The same venue converted to an event friendly space

There were numerous challenges that came up during the 6 week journey leading to the event. The Action Flow Interface chart gave the right direction to planning contingencies and back-up. The Interior teams faced certain challenges and as the event design team, we collaborated well and met with the expectation of the client. The agency interface involved

A View of the site on the morning of the event

- Space Vs. Activity planning to engage guests

The Art of Building Experiential Events

- Thematic flooring and temporary Infrastructure
- Building a Banquet at client site
- Temporary Air con at the venue
- Exclusive Food Lounge and Media Lounge
- Enclosures for Special invitees and State Leaders
- Intelligent day light projection system
- Complete adherence to EHS
- Security plan

d. Event Execution Document With All Inputs and Planning

With wide experience in designing, planning and executing facility inaugurations, the author's agency has specialized infacility inauguration and has handled over 100+ Inaugurations. With time-bound action plans, clockwork precision and a trained team, the presentation is shared encompassing all elements. Shared below is the sample presentation, a real time assignment, which evolves post the discussions with the client team comprising of Communication, Human Resources, Operations team and Head of Business.

1. The opening remark

The EHS Compliance Policy

- Safety of our Workforce
  - All our workforce (both direct & indirect) are covered under WCP
  - We ensure proper & safe transportation of the Workforce at all times
  - Adequate Health Insurance has been taken for the workforce
- Safety at Work site
  - All Workmen involved in Risk exposed activities are provided with safety shoes & helmets
  - Warning gear with safety belts are provided to Workers at Height
  - No Hazardous chemicals or loosely fitted tools are allowed at our work site
- Equipment handling & Management
  - All heavy equipments are shifted using trolleys and capable workforce
  - Electrical units at the sound and lights are only with german sockets
  - No taping of wires / joining of wires are allowed by our management
  - All vehicles have proper documents (Pollution control, Valid Road Tax, Insurance & Licensed
- Workmen Profile
  - All workmen are over the age of 18 and carry ID cards
  - No liquor or smoking is allowed amongst workforce at site
- Human Factor
  - Our operation plan encompasses the Human Factor in all our workings at site for our Workforce as also for our Clients & their Guests

2. The event context

Site Inauguration at the Client (New) Facility

- Where: Location, with address
- When: Date of the event
- Who: (Invitees) Dignitaries, International
- Delegates, Stake holders, Employees, Dealers, Customers.
- Guests: 450–500 pax
- Proposed Time: 09:30 to 13.30 Hrs
- Activity: Site Inauguration

3. Event flow

Inauguration Ceremony – Proposed Flow

Invitees arrive at site (Received & guided to the Event venue thro gate B)	→	Invitees guided to their Seats at the venue (Beverage Counter active)	→	Invitees network by IR Teams at Venue till Ch Guests arrive (Corp Film & Ambience Music)
Sapling Plantation (Brass plates, Planting accessories, Hostess support, Photo Op)	←	Plaque Unveiling (Plaque, Hostess Support, Photo op)	←	Ch Guest & Team guided for Ribbon Cutting (Ribbon décor, Hostess Support & Photo)
Ch Guest & Top Mgmt guided to Cafeteria, Presentation, Walkthro, Demo, Display area	→	Ch Guest & Top Mgmt guided to the event venue (Exclusive Walkway with direct entry near dais with marksmen)	→	Event Commences (Agenda as per client advice)
Refreshments & Take aways (Buffet with casual seating & Take Away Managers)	←	Recognitions/Vote of thanks (Sound, Lights, LED wall, Live)	←	Welcome, Key Note, Plaque Unveiling, making video (Sound, Lights, LED wall, Live)

4. Branding and collaterals

Branding Props – Proposed

Branding Props – (For Discussion & Conclusion)

- Arch at the Main Gate (Box Arch)
- Theme Standees
- Reception/Main Entry – Welcome panel and Pile on
- Direction Boards
  - Parking, Event Area, Food court, VIP Exit , Emergency exit board
- Branding Pile on
  - Legacy of Ingersoll Rand…Each pile on depicting each era…with images at the walk to the event venue.
- Dais , Backdrop, Side Panels, Masking for projections, Skirts for dais
- Wish board
  - A board which is signed by Ch Guest & Select guests and used as a Memorabilia
- Sapling Board
  - Engraved in Brass with poles
- Show and Tell (Display Ideation for the Business Panels) – 4 displays
  - Inauguration Plaque
  - Granite engraved/Burnt Steel finish

5. The venue entrance perspective

While designing the entrance arch at the venue, care is taken to follow norms laid down by the safety teams of the agency and also the client. The arch is designed on the following principles

1. Approved structure designs by the local Government authorities

2. Clear passage way for fire tenders/ ambulance to enter and exit venues in case of emergency

3. Adequate height to facilitate entry of buses/coaches

4. Brand designs aligned

5a. Reference snap of an arch

6. Activity plan

A detailed explanation of the activity and the props spec is shared with the client and a written validation is captured to proceed with the designing of the event.

6a. Activity

- The Leadership team is received with Bouquets (Ambience Traditional Indian Welcome Music)

- Site Anchors to guide guests for the Ribbon cutting, Plaque Unveiling & Sapling

- Ribbon Cutting – Red col Satin Ribbon tied at the entrance with special music played

The Art of Building Experiential Events

- Plaque Unveiling: Specially designed Mobile Kiosk with Brass/Granite plaque & floral decors

- Plant Sapling – at the identified spot

Props

- Ambience Music at the Portico

- Bouquet kept ready to receive Ch Guest & Guest of Honor (qty to discuss)

- Floral & fabric décor at the Lobby , floral Rangoli

- Tables laid for water bottle – Kinley, Aquafina

- Welcome Pile-on branding

- EHS – corner – Safety brochures, First Aid kit, and emergency contact Nos.

- Site Anchors to guide guests to the event venue

ID Cards – Badges Event Specific

- Id Cards for Guests Event based – Optional

- Badges to have the Safety tips & emergency call numbers on the reverse

7. The office entrance

(Ribbon Cutting; decorated entrance way with Ribbon and cutting accessories, ambience music to suit the occasion and Plaque Unveiling (Brass/Granite/Burnt Steel plaque fixed on a mobile kiosk with new linen and floral décor (option of either motorized or manual is proposed).

7a. Reference snaps are shared to commence ideation

Reference samples of the possible treatment of the "First Connect" points are shared with the client and a discussion ensues to arrive at the best option for the project in discussion.

Each assignment has unique points which need to be addressed while designing the event, some corporate subscribe to "Simplicity," while few endorse "Grandeur," it is the responsibility of the design agency to offer the right solution that is aligned to the client belief.

8. Plaque unveiling and sapling planting

These are 2 activities that mark the inauguration of the facility. These 2 components stand testimony to the memorable date of the event as this carries the detail of the guest who inaugurated the facility as also a mark of respect to the environment a sapling is planted.

The agency can offer numerous value add in these areas, like offering real time and virtual plaque inauguration which can be connected with guests around the Globe. Special efforts, by involving horticulturalists, help in identifying the plant that would be suitable for the designated venue.

The VIP is also given an on spot framed photograph soon after the above 2 activities are done and this in itself has been well received in the Corporate Facility Inaugurations.

8a. Reference snaps of Plaque Unveiling and Plant Sapling

The Art of Building Experiential Events

9. Plaque unveiling	**10. Plant sapling**
• Black Granite with sprinkled golden dots/Burnt Steel Finish • Polished to perfection • Letters as per House Colors • Content to be provided by the client • The Plaque to be fixed on a panel to unveil • Time required for the Plaque is 10 working days	• Identify the location (client) • Evaluate options for saplings (to be proposed by Agency Landscape team) • Pit to be dug of 1ft/1ft/1ft • Accessories for the Sapling (Plant kits, towels, shovel) • Red Carpet alongside the aisle of the pits (event agency) • Name Boards – Brass at the sapling points (event agency)

As a good corporate practice, the agency team shares inputs on areas where it would work on, thereby, giving the client a "hands-off" experience. The sample of the agency inputs are shared below

1. Infrastructure support from the agency	**2. Stage décor**

• At the Entrance
  – Red carpet
  – Red and White Satin Flags on poles (to bring the celebration feel)
  – Standees leading to the Site from the main road and over bridge
  – Floral Décor and Bouquets
• At the Welcome Point
  – Welcome tables
  – Arabian Tents at strategic point (near sapling and for the waiting area)
• At the Event Venue
  – Floor Red carpets
	• Virtual LED wall with watch out projection for multi-screen options and Brandings.
	
	• Floral Décor to match the theme on the stage.
	
	• State-of-the-art Sound and lights for the events.
	
	• Plasma screens for delay projection.
	
	• Hostess and Runner supports during Q&A (optional).
	
	• Stage to have Head Tables, Name Cards and accessories.
	
	• Stage lights to suit the ambience and House Color of the company.

- Lycra Chairs with Gold Sash; Head Table chairs and Tea Tables
  - Long tables, Bullard's, Aisle marks
  - Reserved cards, Flex Side walls
  - Round tables, fans, Air Conditioners (tower)
  - Floral décor at the dais
- At the Food Lounge
  - Round Tables with cushion chairs with white linen and Gold sache
  - Tall Tables for Business Lunch
  - Water Tables

- Round Table Seating.
- Red Aisle Carpet.
- Earmarked seats for special invitees.
- Standees to suit the occasion with Theme message and caption.
- Plaque Unveiling sequence.
- Unveiling Mechanism.
- Tables for Beverages on the go.
- Special finish chairs for the head table.
- Beverage managers for serving the Special invitees.
- Innovative stage brand props.
- Branded mic podium.
- Timer panel for the VIP's.
- Tower Air Con and Coolers.

3. Show & Tell

(This is a display on the businesses at the pre-function area of the event venue)

- Each Booth would have a branded walls – Centre and Side panels
- Plasma with VGA and USP port to play Videos/Presentation
- Red/Grey carpet
- Spot lights
- Brochure stand (optional)
- Fabrication Spec:
  - * The Walls are fabricated with Wooden panel with Printed Flex skin

3a. Reference

The Art of Building Experiential Events

- Plasma mounted – on the walls of the panels with DVD and Pen drive support.

- Spot lights and illumination for the display, placing the visual panels a minimum of 40" from the ground aids in excellent viewer experience.

4. Stage view/perception.

5. Other supports

- Professional Master Of Ceremony
  - MC Selection docket would be submitted

- Hostess for the Dais support and Registration

- Site Managers for quick turn-around of event requirements

- Professional Photographer
  - To cover Event
  - For group Photography

- Professional Videographer (Multi-Feed)
  - Static camera
  - Roving Camera
  - Online Editing

e. 2D Drawing and 3D Perspective

After the inputs of the soft issues of the events are discussed, details of the venue are presented and a 2D and 3D design is shared with the client and the final approved layout is handed over to the operations team for execution. Along with the layouts an exhaustive checklist of actions are also discussed and recorded for action. The 2D layout gives details of measurements and dimensions, while the 3D gives an artistic view of the designs, which gives the client the ability to appreciate the creative thought that goes behind the design.

The operations team comes with a top view of the proposed set up incorporating all the requirements that have been discussed and concluded over the series of meetings and exchanges that have taken place. A sample of a layout is illustrated below. A careful observation would help understand the details of props/collateral that gets incorporated.

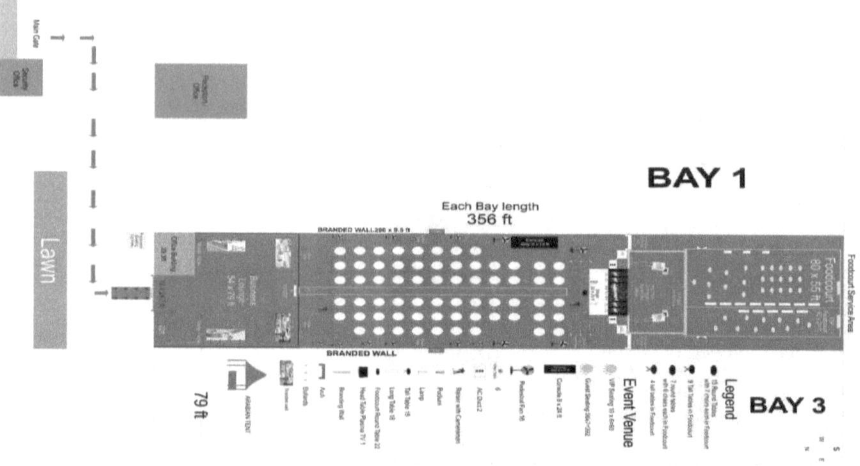

Layout of the event venue with details of props and seating

A line drawing of the venue with dimensions is done by the operations team and is shared with the client and a validation is obtained prior to firming up the requirement. A signed document is exchanged with the client to ensure absolute understanding of the way the set up is being planned by all the stakeholders.

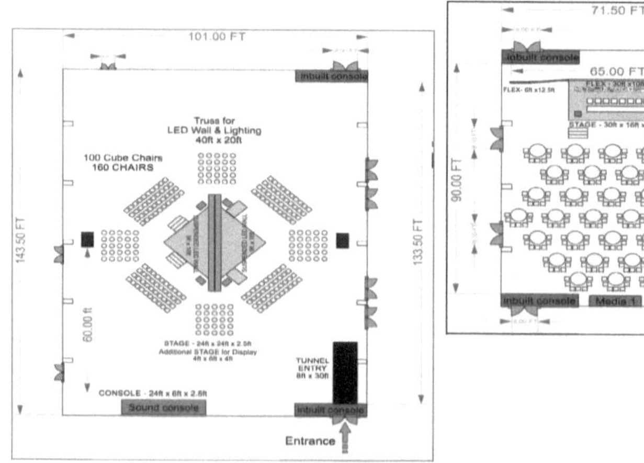

The Art of Building Experiential Events

3D perspective designs, presented below are property of the author and are purely shared for "reference purposes" only

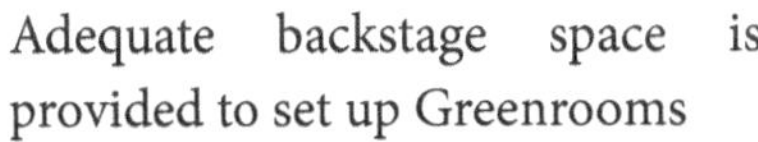

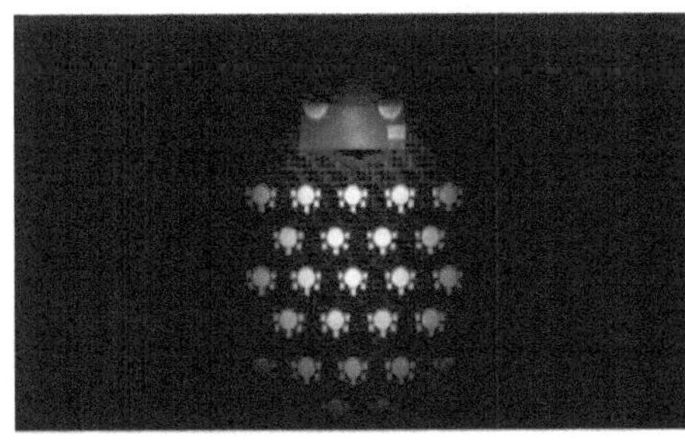

The stage perspective presented is part of a Global Summit and the treatment of Colours, are aligned to the brand guideline.

The backdrop used here is a latest technology projection which is dynamic and moderates around the Brand Persona and greatly helps in breaking monotony

A top view of the Dais is shared for the client to understand the space and the width (dimensions are shared vide 2D for reference).

The stage is multi-level and has fluorescent highlighters that have subtle glow, which aids guests alight and get on to the dais even in dim lighting.

Adequate backstage space is provided to set up Greenrooms

A top view of the 3D is also developed to scale which maps the seating plan for the invitees.

Every action in an event is a Science. The space for a round table is approximately 150 sqft to seat 7 guests seated in comfort on a round table.

The author has mapped such nuances for every customer interface point and the design team fuses these into the final layout development

f. Action List and Execution Plan

A professional agency brings to the table tremendous value to an event, backed by rich experience and professional expertise. The design agency role is not just creating impactful designs but in designing a holistic experience that presents the assignment as a craft of an "Extraordinaire."

The agency need to spend quality time on each project and the proof of the effort is in partly educating, hand holding and training the client teams in running an event successfully. Presented below is one such detailed list of actions that is an important spoke in event designing.

Date: Doc: v2/IR/year

Site inauguration client: global manufacturing unit				
No	Action	Event agency	Others	Comments
A	**Logistics**			
1	Vehicles for the pickup based on group size			guests will come on their own
2	Stickers for branding of the vehicles			NA
3	Putting up of stickers on the vehicle			NA
4	Beverage, newspaper in the vehicle			NA
5	Music in the vehicle from departure point to arrival point			NA
6	Contact number of the driver for Vehicle Tracking			TBD closer to the event day
7	Route plan for travel (briefing to the vehicle drivers)			TBD closer to the event day
8	Arrival and dropping point at site (identify spot)			Imp – TBD – shared responsibility
B	**Welcome at site**			
1	Welcome drink (choice to be discussed)			Do we need this?
2	Cold towels for guests			Do we need this?
3	Ambience music (traditional or fusion to be discussed)			

		company norms	
4	Cafeteria support		Can we look at options?
5	Assembling point guides		
6	Providing safety kits		What will this have?
7	Registration desk management with badges, handing over safety kits etc.		There will be no badges, visiting cards bowl and registration desk
8	Guiding guests to the event venue		
9	Seating plan in the event venue		
10	Name cards for the Chairs (If required)		Not required for the inauguration
11	Colour sash for the chairs (demarcation for the chairs) – If required		TBD
C	**Dais and props, event support**		
1	Dais with white flooring, steps		
2	Arch at the main gate		Measurements for creative development
3	Welcome standees		How many? And Where?
4	Pile ons (assembly, parking, direction boards)		Will these have branding? **NO**
5	Theme standees (business specific)		How many? And Where?
6	Branded mic podium		Measurements for creative development
7	Bullards with chains (queue managers)		
8	Backdrop as per client CIP		Measurements
9	Side panels		Basis our design, we don't need this. Can discuss

10	Screens with branded panels	Measurements
11	Black masking on the backside of the props	
12	Flex and vinyl walls to demarcate the event venue	
13	Sound and lights	
14	LED wall for the projections	Where is this?
15	Wish board for the guests	Not needed
16	Power sockets and connections for the media (optional)	No Media is invited
17	Photography for the event – professional camera	One or two?
18	Videography for the event (multi-camera set up with non-linear edit)	
D	**Moderator & Manpower**	
1	Support for moderator (internal)	
2	Lady hostesses and attire – **sarees in uniform colour**	How many are we looking at and where will they be?
3	Male stewards and attire – **neat full shirts and trousers**	How many are we looking at and where will they be?
E	**Design support**	
1	Creative inputs	
2	Requirement chart apart from the props mentioned above	
3	Guidelines for event related designs.	We need one map of the event venue to be shared with the ELT highlighting the important places that they will be going to through the day.

F	**Infrastructural support**	
1	Head table chairs (7–8 pax)	We don't have any seating on the dais
2	Tea tables for dais	We don't have any seating on the dais
3	Floral décor on the dais **(white, red and green)**	We need to freeze this well in advance
4	Aisle carpet for guests to walk to the venue	
5	Tables at the venue (F&B team to provide glasses, beverages, water, toffees at the event tables) (F&B team to provide flower vase, cutlery, crockery, beverages at the food court)	How many?
6	Cushion chairs for the guests	
7	Traditional lamp with 5 wicks and accessories **(client to come back)**	We'll need 10 wicks – possible?
8	Dust bins with disposable covers	
9	Wash basins with water refills	
G	**Plaque unveiling**	
1	Granite stone plaque (size 2ft ht X 3ft width)	
2	Unveiling mechanism for the plaque at the reception	Manual
3	Detail for the engraving	Can you share some draft content for this?
4	Plaque logistics	
5	Post inauguration fixture of the plaque	
6	Virtual plaque unveiling	Need to discuss this to understand

H	**Statutory**	
1	Fire Engine	
2	Ambulance with nurse support	
3	Fire extinguishers	
4	Security	
5	Valet parking with drivers and car tags	
I	**Food and beverages**	
1	Welcome drink	
2	Water counters	
3	Beverage cans at event venue pre-served	
4	Buffet lunch at the dining hall	
5	Reserved seating for the VIP and media	
6	Menu to be decided	
7	Coffee/tea/fruit juice to be available	
8	Ambience music at the lunch room	
J	**Plant sapling**	
1	Saplings (variety, tropical capability)	Will this be sourced by us?
2	Name boards design for the sapling	
3	Details for the sapling boards	What would be the draft content here?
4	Accessories for the sapling	What would this include?
5	Digging of the pit for the sapling	Who will lead this?
6	Walkway carpet for the sapling	
K	**Tour of the facility**	
1	Tour managers	
2	Grouping of the guests	
3	Pre-plan walk way	

The Art of Building Experiential Events

4	Safety brandings at appropriate points	
5	Timed tour to be done with a recce	
L	**Take away**	we need to finalize this asap
1	Finalize take-aways (theme sketch)	
2	Procurement and logistics for take away	
3	Branded paper bags	
4	Distribution point to be finalized	
5	Managers for the take away distribution (for personalized courtesies)	
M	**Office inauguration**	
1	Ribbon cutting at the admin office	
2	Welcome music (traditional indian music)	
3	Hostess support with scissors	
4	Photographer for capturing the moment	
5	Traditional lamp with 5 wicks with floral décor	
N	**Branding at the pre-event area**	
1	Flex panels with front illumination	
2	Steel frames with tightened flex on the panels	
3	4 panels in total at the pre-event area	

Apart for the list of actions, to be executed, there shall also be a list of responsibility that is conveyed and discussed with the client. Many a times, a less experienced design agency, fails to capture the chart of division of responsibility which can lead to chaos and non-performance on the D-Day. The author and his team have evolved a comprehensive responsibility chart which is run through all the heads of the client event committee.

Site Inauguration
Client: Global Manufacturing

No	Action	Event Agency	Others
A	**Logistics**		
1	Vehicles for the pickup based on group size		✓
2	Stickers for branding of the vehicles	✓	
3	Putting up of stickers on the vehicle		✓
4	Beverage, newspaper in the vehicle		✓
5	Music in the vehicle from departure point to arrival point		✓
6	Contact number of the driver for vehicle tracking		✓
7	Route plan for travel (briefing to the vehicle drivers)		✓
8	Arrival and dropping point at site (identify spot)		✓
B	**Welcome at site**		
1	Welcome drink (choice to be discussed)		✓
2	Cold towels for guests		✓
3	Ambience music (traditional or fusion to be discussed)	✓	
4	Assembling point guides		✓
5	Providing safety kits		✓
6	Registration desk management with badges, handing over safety kits etc.	✓	
7	Guiding guests to the event venue		✓
8	Seating plan in the event venue		✓
9	Name cards for the chairs (if required)	✓	
10	Colour sash for the chairs (demarcation for the chairs) – if required	✓	
C	**Dais and props, event support**		
1	Dais with white flooring, steps	✓	
2	Arch at the main gate	✓	

3	Welcome standees
4	Pile ons (assembly, parking, direction boards)
5	Theme standees (business specific)
6	Branded mic podium
7	Bullard with chains (queue managers)
8	Backdrop as per client CIP
9	Side panels
10	Screens with branded panels
11	Black masking on the backside of the props
12	Flex and vinyl walls to demarcate the event venue
13	Sound and lights
14	LED wall for the projections
15	Wish board for the guests
16	Power sockets and connections for the media (optional)
17	Photography for the event – professional camera
18	Videography for the event (multi-camera set up with non-linear edit)
D	**Media bay (to be discussed)**
1	Exclusive seating for the print and electronic media
2	Press kits
3	On spot photos for the press
4	Press releases
5	Vernacular language of the press releases
6	Client engagement manager for the media
7	Courtesy lounge for the press
8	Gifts for the press
9	Corporate hand-outs
E	**Moderator & Manpower**
1	Support for moderator (Internal)
2	Lady hostesses and attire

3	Male stewards and attire
F	**Design support**
1	Creative inputs
2	Requirement chart apart from the props mentioned above
3	Brand guidelines for event agency to develop designs
G	**Infrastructural support**
1	Head table chairs (7–8 pax)
2	Tea tables for dais
3	Floral décor on the dais
4	Aisle carpet for guests to walk to the venue
5	Tables at the venue
6	Cushion chairs for the guests
7	Traditional lamp with 5 wicks and accessories
8	Dust bins with disposable covers
9	Wash basins with water refills
H	**Plaque unveiling**
1	Granite stone plaque (size 2ft ht X 3ft width)
2	Unveiling mechanism for the plaque at the reception
3	Detail for the engraving
4	Plaque logistics
5	Post inauguration fixture of the plaque
6	Virtual plaque unveiling (Developing 3D plaque with client validation)
I	**Statutory**
1	Fire engine
2	Ambulance with nurse support
3	Fire extinguishers
4	Security
5	Valet parking with drivers and car tags

J	**Food and beverages**
1	Welcome drink
2	Water counters
3	Beverage cans at event venue pre-served
4	Buffet lunch at the dining hall
5	Reserved seating for the VIP and media
6	Menu to be decided
7	Coffee/tea/fruit juice to be available
8	Ambience music at the lunch room
K	**Plant sapling**
1	Saplings (variety, tropical capability)
2	Name boards design for the sapling
3	Details for the sapling boards
4	Accessories for the sapling
5	Digging of the pit for the sapling
6	Walkway carpet for the sapling area
L	**Tour of the facility**
1	Tour managers
2	Grouping of the guests and appointing a leader for the tour
3	Pre-plan walk way
4	Safety Brandings at appropriate points
5	Timed tour to be done with a recce
M	**Take away**
1	Finalize take-aways (theme sketch)
2	Procurement and logistics for take away
3	Branded paper bags
4	Distribution point to be finalized
5	Managers for the take away distribution (for personalized courtesies)

Closer to the event, a master list of actions of important stake holders is drawn with defined deliverables and time lines and an agency quality manager acts as a whistle blower to escalate issues if a task is not completed in accordance to the quality and defined time.

Client: MNC
Chennai Manufacturing Facility Inauguration
19th, 20th And 21st March Checklist

No	Description	Event agency	Client	F & B partner	Date
1	Process for materials and equipment entry and exit after the event				12.03.
2	Hand over bay 3 and Bay 4 fully cleaned for set up				15.03.
3	Permissions for dumping materials from 16th march	mail to Client	permissions		11.03.
EHS props					
	Arranging fire engine and ambulance for 20th March				
	Fire engine letter				11.03.
	Fire extinguisher at the venue/ food court/reception; decision on numbers, placement and energizing if need				19.03.
4	Ambulance				11.03.
5	Floral décor set up at the venue reception – rangoli, lamp décor, stage garden, bouquet				19.03.
6	**Granite plaque – design and production**				
7	Take delivery of granite stone and hand over to client				13.03.
8	Fixing the granite plaque stone				
9	Fabrication of the unveiling – truss with flex and floral décor				18.03.
Plant sapling 14 names – brass boards with brass stem					
10	Organize for the plant sapling boards 14 nos				11.03.
11	Handing over of the brass sapling board to the client				16.03.

12	Organizing the sapling, pre-dug pits and placing the sapling	16.03.
13	Briefing of the placement of brass sapling at the dig – in order of hierarchy	18.03.
14	Accessories for the saplings to be kept ready (shovel, water jugs,	19.03.
15	Accessories for the saplings are ready (tray, gloves, tissue papers, sanitizer)	19.03.
16	Fixing the sapling name boards in the sapling area (14 nos	19.03.
17	Hostess and stewards – sapling support – briefing, action (handing over the accessories to the guest during the event)	20.03.
18	Arabian tent for the area – set up at the site near the sapling area	19.03.
19	Mail regarding security and housekeeping	12.03.

Appreciation props – 14 with names and 5 blankpine wood citation

| 1 | **Organize the appreciation awards (19 nos)** | 09.03. |
| 2 | Handover the awards to the client – Chennai | 17.03. |

Take away gifts – sunflower painting – framed – recycle paper box and branded bag

1	**Take away paintings – 200 nos**	09.03.
2	Receipt of the take away	18.03.
3	Shipping the take away to the site	19.03.
4	Placement of gifts at the take away counter – reception after the event and facilitate – handing over to the guest – with hostess support	20.03.

5	Supervision of handing over of the gift to the guest when leaving		20.03.

Fabrication ref the prop checklist sent

1	**E-mail list of props that would reach the site to the security**		12.03.
2	Shipping of fabrication material at site		16.03.
3	Stage, backdrop, and other elements, side walls, pre event lounge, business panels., side walls in food court		16.03.
4	Power for the pre-lounge area		16.03.
5	Power for the event venue		16.03.
6	Set up of sound console (4 long tables, masking)		18.03.
7	**Infrastructure**		
7.1	Round tables, chairs, long tables, round tables for water counters, tables for the collection point, tables for the appreciation awards. Two lamps on the stage		18.03.
7.2	Water, mint on the first tables		20.03.
7.3	Water bottles on the water tables		20.03.
7.4	Red carpet for the event venue, food court, ELT walkway entry to food court.		18.03.
7.5	AC for the event venue		16.03.
7.6	Pedestal fans		18.03.
7.7	Masking for the AC's		18.03.
7.8	Power for the AC units		17.03.

Infrastructure support for the food court

8	**Shipping to the venue**		18.03.
9	Round tables, chairs, long tables, round tables for water counters		19.03.

10	Give requirements for the food counter (tables, round tables)			11.03.
11	Client to validate the requirements on furniture			
12	Arrange for the tables and round tables			
13	Dustbins and wash basins for food court			19.03.
14	Water bottles for the water counters			20.03.
15	Name cards are placed in the 15 tables for the ELT & ILT team			20.03.

Cafeteria – business session

16	**set up of the Cafeteria**			19.03.
16.1	Infrastructure support (round tables, chairs, long table)			19.03.
16.2	Hand over venue for set up			18.03.
16.3	Power for the venue (approx. 5 kva)			18.03.
16.4	Projections, basic sound, mics at the cafeteria			19.03.
16.5	Water, mint on the tables			20.03.

Reception set up

17	Reception desk, fish bowl, visitors book, pen			19.03.
17.1	Decorated lamp ready			19.03.
17.2	Takeaways for guests (to be arranged and handled)			20.03.
17.3	Red ribbon for cutting, tray with accessories (scissors)			20.03.
17.4	Basic sound system – speakers for playing traditional			19.03.
17.5	Power for the reception area (3 kva)			19.03.
17.6	Guest support tables placed at the walkway area from the business lounge to the event area			19.03.

No.	Task	Date
17.7	Tables are put on place with accessories	
17.8	Welcome courtesies	19.03.
17.9	Marksman from the client to man the PPE counter	19.03.

Pre-lounge Area

No.	Task	Date
18	**Pre-Lounge area set up**	18.03.
18.1	Business panels 4 nos with spot lights energized	18.03.
18.2	Power for the area	18.03.
18.3	Water counters (3 nos)	19.03.
18.4	Water bottle for the counters	20.03.

Projections for the event

No.	Task	Date
19	**Projections set up at the cafeteria and main venue**	19.03.
19.1	LED wall arrival at site	19.03.
19.2	Set up of LED wall	19.03.
19.3	Power for the LED wall	19.03.

Sound & Lights

No.	Task	Date
20	Arrival of sound and light team	19.03.
20.1	Set up of sound and lights	19.03.
20.2	Power for the sound light	19.03.
20.3	Recap – sound set up in 3 locations – event venue, reception area two speakers and delay speaker outside the reception, cafeteria, and additional speakers in food court.	19.03.

Trial run at the event venue 19th march at 4 pm

No.	Task	Date
21	**MC briefing, creating a docket and rehearsal**	
22	Plaque unveiling	19.03.
23	3D Launch	19.03.
24	Sound and lights check	19.03.

The Art of Building Experiential Events

25	Time the activities from the leadership team entering the site, to ribbon cutting, plaque unveiling, sapling, cafeteria, product display zone, business lounge, production bay and enter the event venue		19.03.
26	**External brandings**		
27	Flags – Starting wall of the facility to the main arch – fixing		19.03.
28	Direction boards from (MWC office to site) 10 nos – fixing		19.03.
29	Welcome board – one at 30ft from the gate and one at the reception portico		19.03.
30	Product display standee – before the display area	validation	19.03.
31	**Event day 20.03.**		20.03.
32	Check the direction boards are in place		20.03.
33	Name cards are there in the sapling area		
34	Traditional music is played in the sound system		
35	Ribbon is tied to the door		
36	Reception desk in place with the 2 hostess, bouquets ready, lamp is lit.		
37	One hostess ready with the tray for ribbon cutting		
38	Two hostess ready with the tray for sapling area, the second hostess after the ribbon cutting moves to the sapling area		
39	One hostess from the reception desk will be near the plaque unveiling and then go to the event venue		

40	After sapling another hostess moves to event venue for lamp lighting
41	One hostess will move to the collection point near event venue to receive the PPE's
42	One hostess will be there at the reception desk
43	Supervise awards giving at the stage
44	Appreciation awards are placed near the stage, two hostesses will support here.
45	Stewards – one at the reception, one at sapling area one at the PPE points, one near the stage. After unveiling and sapling is done, two boys will move in. One will be at the reception throughout.
46	Check the podium mic and lapel mic
47	Water is placed in all water counters, water bottles and mint in the cafeteria, the first 4 round tables
48	Food counters are set up
49	Power for food court
50	Name card are placed in the 15 round tables in food court
51	Photographer brief and marksman – moving camera and
52	Final sound projection check
53	Projection and sound system up and running in cafeteria
54	Backstage support
55	Ensure no sound comes from the food court

56	**POST EVENT**	20.03.
56.1	Wind up of teams	
56.2	Fabrication team dismantling	
56.3	Sound & light team dismantling	
56.4	LED wall dismantling	
56.5	Infrastructure set up dismantling	
56.6	Remove external branding	
56.7	Hand over venue to client	
56.8	Take acknowledgment from client regarding hand over of venue intact	

AT the hotel banquets – leadership conference 19th, 20th and 21st

	RESORT	18.03.
1	Permission to place the welcome standee in reception	
2	Venue for set up on 18th night	
3	Set up of stage, backdrop and elements	
4	Sound & light set up on 18th night	
5	Green room set up 18th night	
6	Welcome standee and brandings in place on 19th	
7	Set up of conference venue as per clients requirements 12 round tables and 84 chairs, water, mint, note pad, pencil on the tables	
8	Set up of the 3 break away rooms as per requirements	
9	Breakaway rooms – Nautica on U shape seating for 35 captains table and managers meeting room	
10	Check sound & light and be ready for 19th meeting	19.03.

11	Plasma TV with VGA cord, in managers meeting room on all 3 days (19th, 20th and 21st)		
12	Wind up on 19th night after the meeting is over		
13	Dinner is ready at infinity pool side		
14	Shuttling guests to the dinner venue		19.03.

20th March at hotel banquets

15	20th morning be ready with the sound and light set up		
16	Ensure the banquet set up is ready as per clients requirements in all 4 venues		
17	Ensure the tea and coffee break timing are adhered to by the banquets team		
18	Sound and lights check up for evening entertainment		
19	MC briefing, creating a docket and full rehearsal		
20	Arrival of artistes on 20th evening		
21	Tea coffee snacks for artistes		
22	Artistes to be ready for the show on time		
23	Wind up of special lights & sound after event on 20th		
24	Dinner to be ready at lawns		20.03.
25	Shuttling guests to the dinner venue		20.03.

21st march at hotel banquets

| 26 | Ensure sound & lights are checked and fine | | |
| 27 | Banquets set up as per clients requirements in all 4 venues | | |

The Art of Building Experiential Events

28	Wind up after the event on 21st
29	Dismantling of fabrication
30	Dismantling of sound & light

Miscellaneous support from the client
Housekeeping on 19th and 20th
Security – 18, 19th and 20th
Restrooms: Housekeeping, direction route boards, and lighting
Logistics plan – Identifying car park location, safety instructions,

g. VIP Protocol and Management

A table of the VIP protocol management is drawn out mapping details and ensuring the event flow progresses without any hitch. Once the protocol is mapped, the agency team nominates anchors who would monitor action the deliverables. It is prudent to have wireless communication sets for the agency heads to be on top of the situation, lest there be a slip up.

Select points to keep in focus when senior state leaders attend an event. The role assumes significance as the safety wing and venue security will be tightened and hence all necessary planning needs to be done ahead as last minute requests will be turned down by the state security department.

No	Points to be in focus	National leader	State leader	Senior bureaucrat
1	Site work completion and handover	24 hours prior	12 hours	3–6 hours prior
2	Badge for event workforce	Photo ID; validated	Photo ID	Agency ID
3	Security agency	Government appointed	Government appointed	Approve security agencies
4	Validation of dais/equipment/ exit etc.	Mandatory and if government safety agency is not satisfied, the same need to be redone to their expectation	If the agency is a listed vendor of the government, a check by the authorities will be done and approved	Registered agency of the organizer with a security approval of the police

No	Points to be in focus	National leader	State leader	Senior bureaucrat
5	Focus Areas	Strength of the Dais	Strength of the Dais	Registered agency to share detailed drawings, equipment lists and site head to approve by his authority.
		Sound equipment	Sound equipment	
		Console away from dais	Entry and exit controlled	
		Only approved workforce	Special seats to be blocked	
		Backstage doors locked	Vehicle parking – convoy	
		Entry and exit Controlled	First few rows marked for guests of the state leader.	
		All gifts to be pre-checked		
		Seating protocol as advised	Press enclave clearly marked	
		Special seats to be blocked		
		Emergency marksmen		
		Vehicle parking – Convoy		
		Jammer as advised		
		Press enclave clearly marked		
6	Gift and memento management	Gift is validated by the government security team.	Gift is validated by the state security team.	The organizer and their secretariat take the responsibility.

       The Art of Building Experiential Events

No	Points to be in focus	National leader	State leader	Senior bureaucrat
		The gift is held in safe deposit with a designated manager of the client or the agency.	The gift is held in safe deposit with a designated manager of the client or the agency.	
		The gift is monitored by a guard.		
		The marksman is the only person authorized to carry the gift to the stage.		

Common Points to be addressed

1. Entry and exit to be kept separate for the special guests and the general invitees

2. Also provide separate entry and enclosure for the Media teams and provide ample space for photo and video teams

3. Earmark a space for the online media team who would require a console for posting live tweets

4. Reserve chairs with either name of the dignitaries or post marksman for each reserved seat

5. It is ideal to have an exclusive area for media briefings post or pre-event to get Media Bytes

6. Provide large video monitors for the head table guests with adequate sound fills around the dais

7. A Minimum of 36" of width space to be provided for each chair on the head table.

8. Each guest should have a folder with timed agenda, profile of other guests on dais, notepad and a pencil

9. Water is mandatory and choice of beverage to be planned in consultation with the respective coordinating officer

10. Name card on head table to be in double side and of a readable size

11. Free space behind the head table chairs to be a minimum of 6 feet to facilitate stationing of guards and emergency evacuation

h. Flow of Event and Agenda

Presented below is a typical agenda that is drawn up for the event which is run through the agency heads along with the client anchors to validate before circulating to the ground operation teams.

Here's a sample of a protocol-driven event

Proposed Inauguration Program

Date: monday, date, month and year time: 10:00 to 12:00 Hrs.

Venue: EXPO CONVENTION CENTRE, (500 Guests Theatre style Seating)

Live feed of the inauguration program to be synced to all displays/big screens across venue

Arrival and welcome reception: 09:30–09:45 Hrs.

09:45–10:00 Hrs.	Reception committee to welcome dignitaries at the (protocol lounge team) –Chairman, president, VPs to lead.
	National leader, State leader
	Others – to assemble at the VIP enclosure.
09:45 – 09:55 Hrs.	MC to invite all participants to take their seats.
10:00 – 10:05 Hrs.	At 10:00 hrs, the dignitaries (to be seated on the dias) walk into the Expo hall, MoC invites the dignitaries to the light (special lighter) the lamp and take their seat on the dias (8 seats to be kept vacant in first row for dignitaries during unveiling sequence) Seated on dias – as per protocol.
	Chairman, Welcome address
	President – Presidential address
	State leader – Guest of Honour – Keynote Speech

	National leader,– Chief Guest – Host Speech
	Vice President – Address
Welcome Address 10:05–10:10 Hrs.	MC thanks the dignitaries and invites Chairman, to deliver the welcome address.
President Address 10:10–10:15 Hrs. 10 min	MC thanks and invites President to deliver his presidential address.
Address by Guest of Honour 10:15–10:25 Hrs.	MC thanks President, requests State leader to deliver his address.
	MC thanks the State leader and requests President, to Handover a memento.
Keynote Address Guest of Honour 10:25–10:35 Hrs.	MC invites National leader to deliver his keynote address. MC thanks and requests Chairman to handover a memento.
10:35–10:50 Unveiling Gig	MC invites the special guests, to launch the unveiling gig and declare open the event.
Launch of Print Memorabilia 10:50–10:55 Hrs.	MC invites announces launch of the print memorabilia and hand over the first copy to the Chairman.
Recognition of Organizers. 10:55–11:10 Hrs.	MC requests state leader to recognize the organizing team
	Then MC requests the Chairman and President to Honour the National leader followed and State leader.
Vote of Thanks 11:10–11:15 Hrs.	MC requests VP to propose the vote of thanks.
Guiding guests for media briefing 11:15–11:30	MC requests the guests to remain seated and requests the dignitaries on the dais to join for the media briefing at the "business hall."
Media interactions 11:30–12:00	Media Interactions and 2 one-on-one interviews.
Dias Sequence	1, 2, 3, 4, 5, – VP, Chairman, SL, NL, President

i. Sensitivities Like Playing the National Anthem/Prayer Song

The national anthem represents the culture, belief and heritage of a country and its citizens. It is a treasured treatise and need to be addressed with respect and regard.

Events with national/international participation have a slot for playing the national anthem of the respective countries. When the national anthem is played, the guests stand up as a mark of respect.

The widely experienced author has had interactions with several government heads of various countries and has collected information that pertain to the protocol process that need to be followed while playing a national anthem.

Apart from the above, the unfurling of the national flag too has a specific protocol which needs to be followed. Few important tips that distinguishes a professional design agency is listed below

- A quick "to do" points to be read out by the MC or to be projected on the screens at the venue.

- The MC/host to read out the Respect protocol to be followed and guide guests with instructions.

- Entry and exit to the venue to remain closed while the anthem is played.

- Guests advised to keep their phones on mute mode.

- Avoid covering guests on a camera connected to a screen as this disturbs the guests.

- A good practice is to run the lyrics of the anthem on the screens at the venue.

- Highlight the agenda with the segment on playing of the national anthem.

Religious songs/prayers are also typically part of inauguration events. It is but respectful to study the profile of the attendees before deciding on the prayer song. It is prudent to play non-religious prayer songs or even better to play patriotic opening songs during special ceremonies at the time of inaugurals.

In India, lighting of the traditional lamp signifies commencement of events. The lamp is lit with 5 wicks which represent the 5 elements. The concept of respect to the 5 elements is part the Vedic history and is today a norm across faiths and beliefs in India. True to the Indian spirit the tunes that are non-religious are played during the lamp lighting. Some of the favourite tunes are on the genre of "faith in almighty;" "message of peace;" "wishing prosperity and happiness."

j. Photographer and Videographer Brief

Photographers are visual people, ideally one A4 sheet with bullet points is the best brief as it's simple to retain and refer as the situation arises. The brief to the photographer to be simple and straight as sheets of paper will be more a hindrance than help. When a photographer brief is made it can ideally contain:

- The venue name, address, phone numbers
- Site contact
- Reporting time and set up time
- Site tour and important areas to be covered
- Profile of guests in order of importance
- What happens when and where
- Flow of event and focus area to click
- Quick run on the speakers and their time of speech
- Specials like awards, group photo and candid shots
- Locations for welcome, registration, dinner etc.

If it is not your regular photographer, it is suggested to give out images of the speaker and important participants for them to be covered for sure. If you have a requirement for group shots; list names for each shot, keep it to the minimum possible to ensure time is maintained. Keep a standby photographer for important events as on spot requests could come up and unless the bandwidth is available it can be a challenge.

Categorize the shots based on formal, informal, casual, album and angles. This might list your requirements for a mix of reportage and formal shots for archives. Special briefing to cover the set up including the backdrops, floral arrangements, any special lighting, displays can be included and can be shot either prior or post the event,.

The photographer should be advised to come prepared to colour correct and transfer select shots of the event for the purpose of:

- Handing over a quick print of a celebrated moment to the recipient
- As required by the media
- Posting on social media
- Online media promotions
- Create a live virtual album at the venue during the dinner
- Handover a first cut version to the client at site.

Having recorded the photographer brief as above, it is critical to educate the client on what can be expected soon after the event with regard to the photos that are shot.

Some clients may want every possible snap with nil turn-around time. However it can be a nightmare to copy the entire content as it may be time-consuming. It is recommended to advise clients to look for select shots and take those rather than all the content. There might be requests to transfer more shots with a point that our clients would need shots of guests who turned up early and those who turned up late. In such a scenario, best advised is to work overnight and send out the content vide online.

To capture shots of the guests as they arrive normally will involve the photographer to be placed at the registration counter prior or at the landing point just after registration. This is not a preferred option as this causes problems of guests being uncomfortable if they are still not in their coats or some will head to the cloakroom, so this can be the least favourite option.

To avoid any guest discomfort, there can be a networking spot prior at the pre-function that serves welcome beverages and this could be an ideal spot for capturing the best moments at networking.

To make the event memorable, thematic photo opportunity displays can be planned at the pre-function networking point for guests to spend time to get clicked. Unless there is a fantastic show stopping display that everyone will want to be photographed with at the entrance to your venue; be prepared for queuing and entertaining photograph requests.

Another opportunity to capture the guests is when they are seated at their table. The angles are many and the photographer if experienced, will make the best of an opportune moment. Usually at the table, the guests are at their best

So, the shots turn out well and these would be well appreciated by the guests too.

If one plans to take two shots per table the time it takes can be around a minute and if this has to be repeated for 30 tables, a good 30 minutes has to be allocated, hence in such a scenario having a free roam photographer to capture these moments is advisable.

The Art of Building Experiential Events

k. Unveiling Thought and Plan

Each corporate have their own brand identity and is known as "corporate identity program." The communication team of the corporate have the brand docket which would extensively cover the way the brand has to be presented with details like

- The scientific analysis of brand colours
- The definition of the brand personality
- The concept behind the presentation of a brand
- The style and fonts that represent the brand
- The treatment of the colours across media of exposures
- Vertical/horizontal/bunting style treatment of the brand
- Specific ideations for presentations
- The logo mnemonic with status of registrations/patents etc.
- The sign off line and its positioning

Brand Identity Reference (Reference)

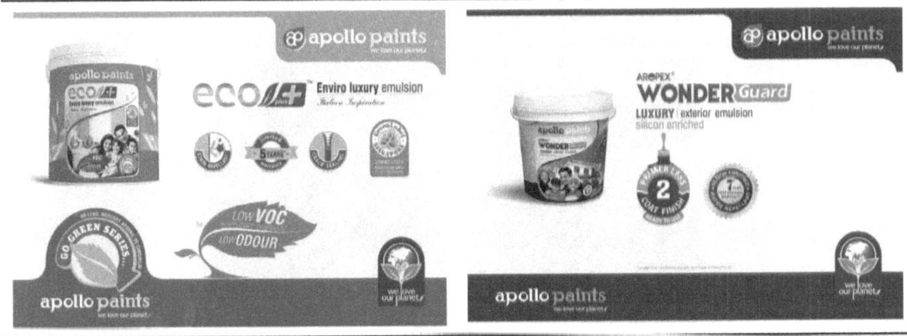

Each brand has a unique identity like the humans, their creation is a factor of the brand objective and it is designed to meet the persona it is to represent.

Logo style (Font and Colour): The logo and the style of writing is evolved in line with a brand purpose. The treatment of the logo in different media is designed based on a detailed application oriented approach. Certain brands dictate strict rules with regard to usage of multiple colours on them, while some brands allow a certain amount of creative deviation. The brand docket or the corporate identity manual is a must for all brands, and leading brands follow the directions without deviation.

The brand docket guides with regard to the following points, which need to be meticulously followed:

- Usage of the logo and the style of depiction
- Spacing of the logo and the size proportionate to the medium of exposure
- Colour schemes with connotation of the scientific mix
- Usage of special images or certifications
- Adaptation of the logo on print/electronic and display mediums
- Any special treatment like a band
- Adaptation of the logo on the outdoor media
- Specific directions towards using the logo on animations and electronic media
- Do's and don'ts

Unveiling using a panoramic screen fusing technology and live performances

The above was done for the unveiling of a global expo where the agency deployed the concept of panoramic screen with live performer interface while unveiling the logo of the said expo. This type of set up, designing & execution, involves extensive planning, coordination and live content management with precision and finesse.

l. Décor and Brand Collaterals aligned to CIP

As explained above, the designs developed for an event, be it facility inauguration or a leadership conclave will need to follow the brand guidelines. Presented below are samples that represent the brand guidelines. The grid below is an illustration of collateral developed for a leadership conclave alongside an inauguration.

The Art of Building Experiential Events

The thought – The wheel architecture, a patent of the Chola Kings (The warriors of Tamil Nadu who spread their might across Asia).

This celebrated antique architecture is fused with trendy infrastructure retaining the "Make In India" "Respect to environment" "Dynamic thinking." An evolution towards progress that the client brand stands for.

The thought – success unlimited

The attributes of the conclave, celebrating the success of the Brand and a promising future with the optimum alignment of innate talents.

m. Entertainment to Suit the Event

The entertainment capsule in a facility inauguration or in a conclave or in any client event is best customized. The option that the design agency proposes should be aligned to the beliefs of the corporate, the fibre of the event, and the profile of the guests and more importantly the entertainment should reflect the corporate objective. The author's agency has commendable experience in designing corporate entertainment that is exclusively created to suit the client requirements.

The following illustration is the concept that was evolved and presented alongside a facility inauguration. The concept brief was as follows:

- A Japanese organization was setting up a state-of-the-art manufacturing facility in India.

- The business category is in automation (industrial and home).

- The inauguration of the facility was done by a bureaucrat.

- The entertainment to be a fusion of Indo-Japanese tradition, or Indian cultural specific capsule.

- The profile of invitees included leading businessmen from the city, journalists, bankers, stakeholders and key customers.

- The duration of the entertainment was capped at 45 minutes.

- There would be service of cocktail and dinner soon after the entertainment.

With the above inputs, the entertainment capsule was conceived and as a standard operating format, the agency would propose 3 options for the client to deliberate and decide. A gist of the entertainment capsule developed for the specific need is shared below.

Event Facts

- The Inauguration event of a Global Manufacturing Giant

- Event Specs
  - The Date : Month, year
  - Venue : New Facility - Asia
  - Event Time : Morning

- The event is to be attended by about 250-300 guests (Global Leadership, Country Leadership, Stakeholders, Unit Colleagues, Special Invitees)

- Develop a 25-30 min entertainment ensemble that would enthrall Indian & Japanese Guests

- The Entertainment sequence will be part of the Inauguration ceremony

Agency Creative – A Theatre Experience

- The agency designing team also specializes in developing exclusive entertainment & Theatre Concepts suiting the theme of the events & profile of Delegates

- The agency has Conceptualized, Developed and Created over 10 Theatre Musicals around Themes Viz.. India, Women Empowerment, Indian Films, Culture & Trade amongst other numerous Client Specific Entertainment capsules.

- The Performances are precise, powerful, interesting & are widely appreciated for the class and Finesse

- The Theatre is a combination of videos, voice over, interactive gigs and colourful performances by specially trained dancers

---

The Art of Building Experiential Events

The Entertainment Thought

- This is a facility by a Japanese Global Giant in India with its strategic location in South India catering to the Asian Market.

- With the new initiatives drawn by the two countries, India is to gain substantially with the technology & Innovation from JAPAN, a country known for its superior technological capabilities.

- Chennai is the Cultural Capital of India & has had deep rooted trade connection with Japan since 6th Century

- The Two countries have been the nerve centre in ASIA for propagating Trade Ties, Religious Ties & Empowerment in the region

- Today Japanese & Indian Arts are exchanged and learnt widely

Entertainment Capsule
(Capturing the Innateness of the Indo-Japanese Culture)

Entertainment Options

RHYTHMSCAPE Rhythm & Percussion Performance	CONFLUENCE Art & Dance	DANCESCAPE Dance Performance
• Powerful Ensemble by Performing Artistes from India & Japan • Japanese Artiste will perform alongside Indian Artistes with the theme of *"Inspiration"*	• An Unique confluence of Art & Dance • A Celebrated Painter to produce live a Thematic Art , alongside a Dance Performance by Indian & Japanese Dancers	• Dance Performance by Professionals • High Energy Dance performed by Indian Dancers to Global Music (Genre includes Indian, Japanese, Western)

Rhythm Ensemble

A Musical Ensemble featuring Popular Musicians from Japan & India
A Band of 3-4 Musicians perform to a Theme that interestingly covers the musical genius of the two cultures..

Image for reference purposes only

CONFLUENCE

A Tribute through Art & Dance on the theme of *"Inspire"* Award Winning Artiste paints a Dedication to the New Facility as Dancers perform & engage the audience.
The Paint storks matches the graceful expressions of the Dancers

This is a wonderful experience where the audience view a love art painted by a Famed Artiste in sync with the dance expressions within a given time frame. Impromptu Art on Canvas by renowned Painter matching the Dance Forms of India and Japan

DANCESCAPE

Professional Dancers, Hand picked from Premier Dance Academy perform for a duration of 20-25 min on a theme.
Performance Varies from Indian Fusion, To Indo-Japanese Fusion
A Group of 10 Dancers will be performing

Scope

Agency	Client
- Artist Selection and Rehearsals - Costume/Makeup/ Training support - Music and props relevant for the act - Timing and logistics of the artist - Direction on the D-Day - Script for the necessary performance - Backend support for Artist performance	- Stage set up as per requirements - Sound and light as per our the Performance rider - Green rooms for the artist - Tech rider with regard to projections - Refreshment for the artist - Rehearsal Time/Demo as prescribed - Any Licenses to be procured by the executing agency

Based on the concept approval the technical rider for sound & light will be shared. Props like raiser, Number of Dancers will be decided based on the Stage Size proposed by the operations team

A 3D Perspective of the venue is also presented to the client. If the venue is open air, 2 views are shared with the client for them to get a perspective of the proposed set up that would feature the entertainment discussed. If the entertainment is planned as a separate activity, then the view is presented encompassing the venue. Presented below is a sample of a view developed by the author's agency for an open air entertainment event alongside a facility inauguration.

 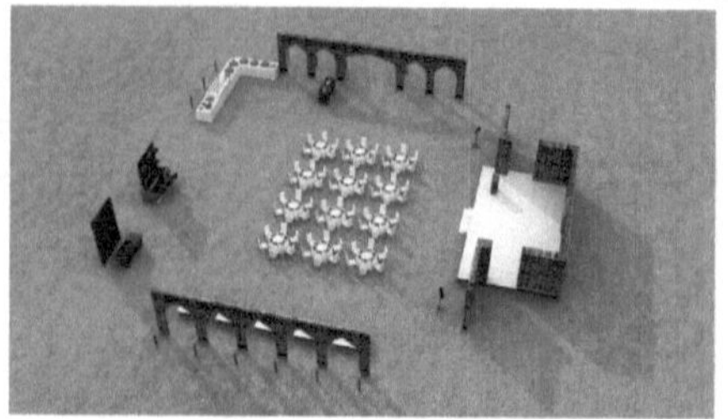

n. Insurance for the Workforce During the Event and for the Event

Personal accident and sudden disposition of the event anchor

Though the event team is fairly large in terms of size, and even though an established agency is fairly organized, it's difficult to be planned for unexpected contingency. There are situations when the key anchor has taken ill at the nth hour. And hence is advisable to insure for sudden disposition and illness/personal accidents.

Professional indemnity insurance by the event design agency

In the course of work as an event design agency, there are possibilities of error or negligence by a team member unknowingly which can lead to a claim by either the client or a third party. The best solution is to engage a professional insurance consultant who would advise a professional indemnity insurance that covers critical financial protection that covers costs towards the claim including any incidental legal charges.

Third party liability insurance

Third party liability insurance is important for event teams, as it will cover for any damage to a person or property in the course of execution of an assignment. Large corporates, demand a copy of these insurance that covers any third party liability if an event is planned for public attendance. There have also been instances of insurance compliances for covering clients who visit event production sites.

General insurance for property of event teams

General insurance for properties that are usually carried to sites for work that include expensive tools, laptops, site measurement apparatus and electronic

                                    The Art of Building Experiential Events

gadgets that are used by the event teams The insurance premium is proportionate to the deprecated value of the said properties.

Tax audit cover

Any professionally managed business has to be completely tax compliant, and in the interest of ethical business practices, it is essential to conduct tax audits which can reveal uncovered expenses. To make sure, that there is adequate coverage for such risks, select insurance companies offer cover at a premium which can be discussed and finalized with professional insurance consultants.

WCP (workmen compensation policy)

Events include service of many contractors and the collective responsibility lies with the event agency who is the nodal force in driving the activity. It is thus very important for the event agency to also cover contractors or site workmen with the workmen compensation policy. The policy is an excellent option that covers accident at site, any mishap or even loss of life. Inspite of the best planning, events can go wrong and it is advisable to have the WCP for the contractors. The event insurance can be taken for a single site for a day or multiple sites for a period of up to 6 months.

o. Permissions, Licenses and Approvals

A separate vertical in the agency functions exclusively on the permissions and requirements. These approvals and permissions are mandatory and can invite penalty for non-adherence.

Some of the permissions that are required for conducting an event is listed below (the requirements mentioned herein are pertaining to events wherein the venue is a hired location or a manufacturing Location)

No	Permission/license	Objective/purpose
1	Police Permissions	Bandobust during the event and parking approvals
2	Public works department/ Pollution control board	Permission for using power back-up and cleaning clearances
3	IPRS	Performing Rights for any musical/entertainment program
4	PPL	Public performance license for use of recorded rights music
5	Fire engine/ambulance	Fire and health department permission to handle an emergency

p. Dismantling and Venue Handover to Clients

The post event handover is an important aspect of any event, as this portrays the professionalism of the design agency. This act of clearing the venue and handing it back over in the same condition as we had taken possession will be appreciated by the client and will help in better bonding between the agency and the client.

The handing over element should be part of the event process and the author's agency has put this into practice which is regarded as a post event service. The HR department and the admin department are involved in the post event clean-up and an effort from the event agency is well appreciated and paves way for a long standing association. Presenting below a sample of the communication sent to the client post the event.

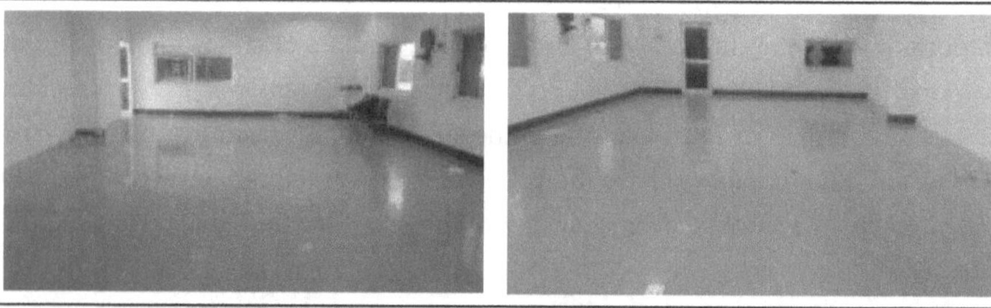

Hi Mr. Joe,

We have cleared the event venue of our materials and nothing is left behind. Please find attached, a photo of the hall. We understand that the housekeeping has also cleared all debris. We have handed over the pen drive with photographs and the AC remote to Shankar. Thanks for the opportunity to work with your teams once again.

When clients shun saying you are expensive, be proud because to be expensive means you have a worth.

– Deepak Swaminathan

Chapter 10

DESIGNING A MUSICAL EVENT FOR PUBLIC AUDIENCE

Designing a musical event or a public gathering event, is a challenging proposition as the stakes involved are high and so are the risks. The process involved in the event design and execution is similar to an event run for a "facility inauguration." There are a few areas that distinguish the public/musical event from a facility/corporate show

a. The Mapping Grid

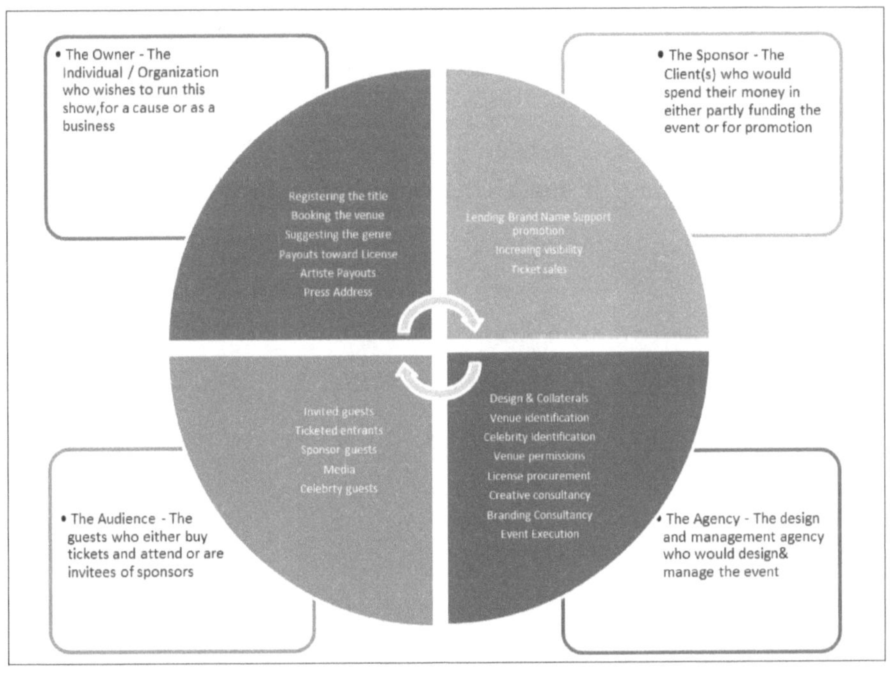

b. Key Pointers for Commencing the Planning

Key Pointers for the Owner
- Appoint the agency from discussion stage
- Estimate the event & its requirements
- Clarity on Objective of the event
- Partner with an NGO, if event is for a cause
- Clarity on permissions & licenses
- Appoint an experienced Lawyer
- Clarity on genre of the event
- Define the target audience
- Identify partners who would bring in value
- Plan of raising initial funding
- Bridge funding for delays in collection
- Register the event and secure ownership
- Appointing Safety officers
- Procuring license toward the temporary construction of structures

Reference points for the partner Agency
- Understand the objective of the event
- Propose celebrity options & event thoughts
- Work on slim pricing
- Identify & sign up sponsors
- Educate the owner on the key actions
- Support in procuring permissions
- Empanelment of Sound, Light engineers
- Venue decor & lighting
- EHS and human factor considerations
- Branding and designing
- Negotiating Venue / Hotel Partners
- Promotion plan and negotiating media partners
- D-Day management and support

c. The Flow Chart of Actions

Presented below is the flow chart of actions while designing a musical/public event. The order of actions and the timelines of execution determine the success of an event.

A public interface event has many challenges in an eventuality leading to further complications to the extent of arrest of the organizer and the designer.

The flow chart below presents a detailed view of the areas in order of importance and captures finer issues that governs the activity as a whole.

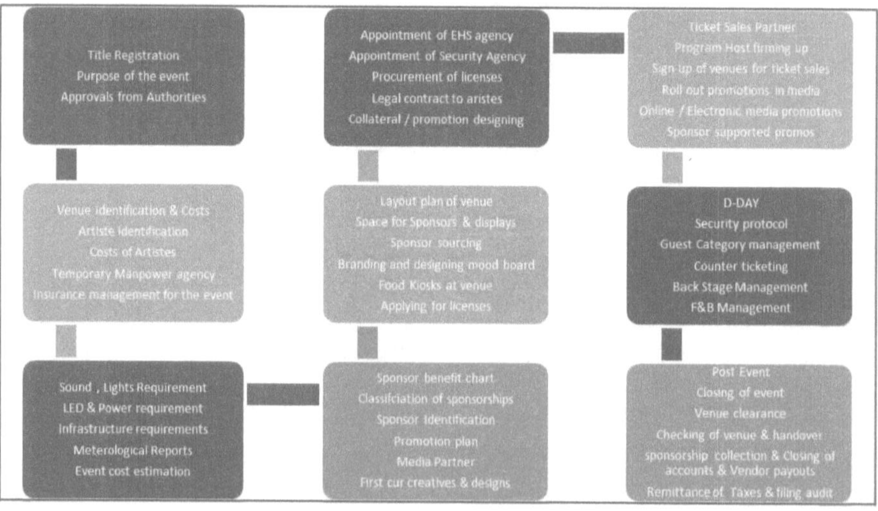

The Art of Building Experiential Events

d. Stage, Sound and Light Management

Every artiste has a specific requirement with regard to the stage design and also the placement of the equipment. While designing the stage and the placement, the design agency, needs to take the following into consideration

1. The number of artistes who would be at the stage at any point of time.

2. The entry and exit to the stage.

3. Designing a wireless experience in human interface areas.

4. The chronology or sequence of equipment to be placed on the dais.

5. The overall lighting plan.

6. The venue perspective vs. the placement of the stage.

7. The entry and exit of the audience and the placement of audio speakers.

8. The distance between each performing artiste.

9. Any special ramp etc. for the main gig that is to be showcased.

10. The green room placement for the celebrity artistes.

11. The projection plan for telecast.

12. The placement of the sound console and management team.

13. F&B area and set up for the guests to network.

14. Placement of gensets and power systems.

15. General illumination and barricading of the venue and stage areas.

16. A sample of the sound support that is prepared based on the Artiste genre.

1. A 4 WAY FOH SPEAKER SYSTEM MUST BE PROVIDED WITH SUFFICIENT POWER TO EVENLY COVER THE ENTIRE VENUE .
2. MUST BE ABLE TO REPRODUCE 115 dB SPL AT FOH POSITION.
3. THE FOH SPEAKER SYSTEM MUST BE RIGGED TO FLY.
4. FOH CONSOLE MUST BE SLIGHTLY OFF CENTRE OF P.A. NOT MORE THAN 80 FEET AWAY FROM THE CENTRE OF THE STAGE.
5. VENUES THAT HAVE MIXING DESKS INSTALLED IN OR UNDER A BALCONY, WE REQUEST ANOTHER MIXING DESK TO BE PLACED IN THE CENTRE OF THE AUDIENCE.
6. THE CONSOLE MUST AT ALL TIMES BE FACING THE STAGE AND NEVER BE SIDEWAYS. AWKWARD CONSOLE POSITIONS WITHOUT GOOD SIGHT OF THE BAND WILL NOT BE ACCEPTED. THE CONSOLE MUST ALWAYS BE ON A RISER. THE CONSOLE MUST HAVE AN OVERHEAD SHADE IN ALL OUTDOOR VENUES.
7. PLEASE THINK BIG, SUB-BASS HEAVY NIGHT CLUB SOUND.
8. WE REQUIRE A MINIMUM OF 3 HOURS OF SETUP AND SOUND CHECK TIME. NO DISTRACTIONS DURING THIS TIME WILL BE TOLERATED.
9. NO PROPS OR DÉCOR BLOCKING THE SPEAKER SYSTEM OR THE FOH CONSOLE WILL BE ALLOWED.
10. ANY LOCAL SOUND LEVEL RESTRICTIONS SHOULD BE INFORMED TO THE MANAGERS AND ENGINEER IN PRIOR.
11. THE BAND RESERVES THE RIGHT TO NOT PERFORM IF ANY OF THESE CONDITIONS ARE IGNORED.
12. ALL SUBSTITUTIONS AND EXCEPTIONS MUST BE APPROVED BY THE ENGINEER MUCH PRIOR TO THE SHOW.

Sr. No.	Topic
1.	PA and MONITORING SYSTEM
2.	INPUT LIST
3.	STAGE PLOT, RISERS, and MONITOR PLOT
4.	BACKLINE REQUIREMENTS

PA and MONITORING SYSTEM

- PREFERED SPEAKER SYSTEM:
- JBL Vertec VT4889 – VT 4880-A
- JBL Vertec VT4888 – VT 4880

STAGE PLOT 2013B

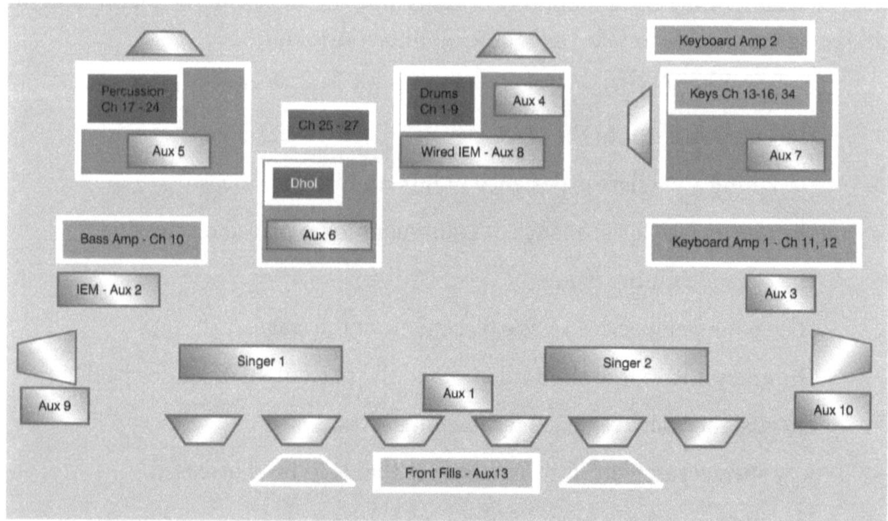

The Venue layout with legend

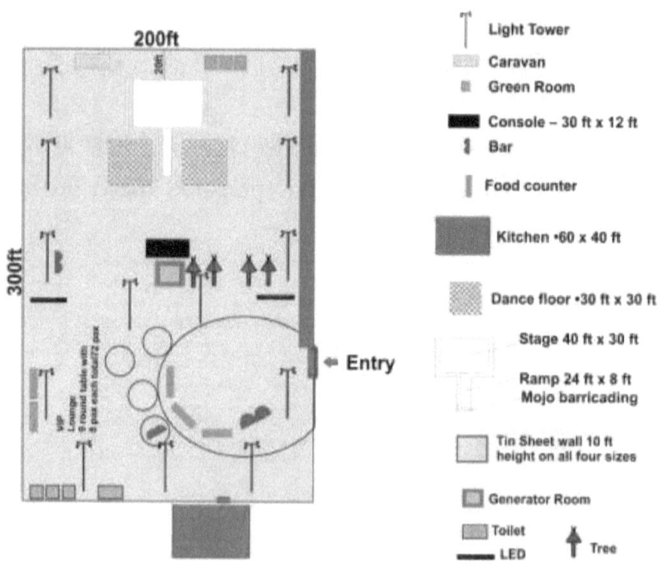

The Art of Building Experiential Events

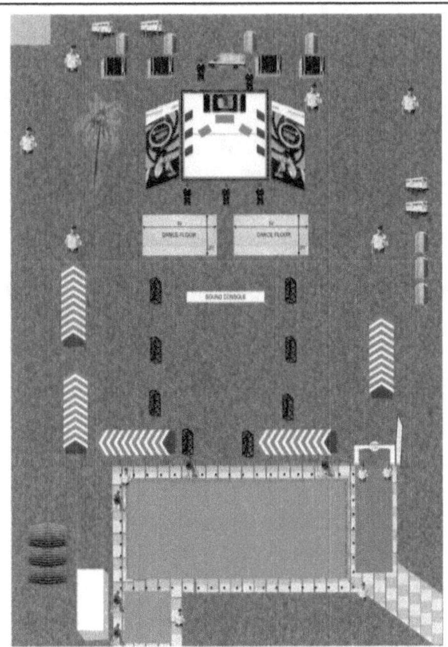

Colour perception of the layout

The client coordination team is appraised of the actions to be taken by the event agency by sharing the following:

- A brief document of what happens, at which time

- Responsibility sheet

- Line drawing of the venue and its perception

- A colour layout for quick understanding

- A detailed specification-oriented drawing for discussing critical inputs

- Ideation on placement of security posts

- Entry for artistes team and other guests

- A perception of the venue and its facilities.

18.   Perception of the stage in a 3D drawing.

Open view of the stage. This shows the skeletal design of the dais with dance floors, side panels and depth in the backdrop for the entry and exit of the artistes and performers.

This drawing indicates the overall layout with side barricades and a grid in the centre depicts either a décor of a projection as may be decided in consultation with the client and entertainment teams.

When a layout is made, the following need to be kept in focus

- The entry and exit of artistes

- The connect points with the guests and the artistes

- Barricades

- Branding opportunities on the dais

- Raisers for any product display

- Dais extensions etc.

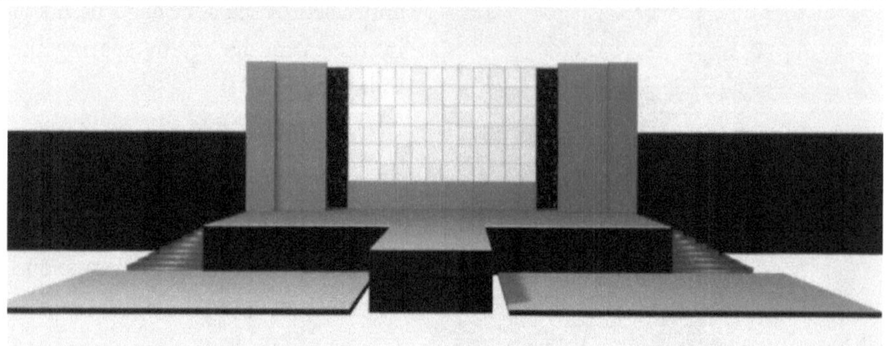

The drawing in detail with specs

The top view of the dais shows the perception of the prop placements. Once this layout is ready, the same is shared with the client with inputs on the prop placements as shown above and the final planning is done.

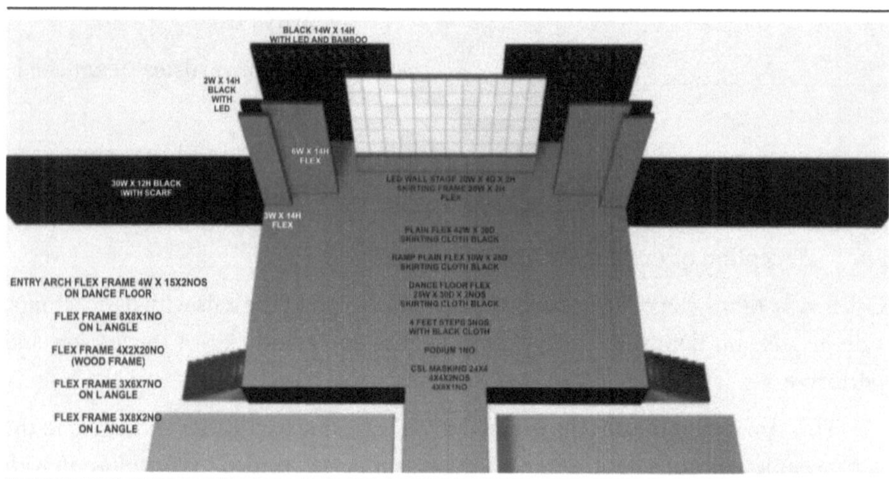

The Art of Building Experiential Events

e. Managing a Crisis or an Incident at the event

Preparedness towards managing an incident

A risk assessment in an event is a good initiative while commencing a plan for an event. This is an area that many agencies overlook, while the experienced ones will never deviate and the value of which is felt only when an occasion arises.

This will help you focus on areas that will need to be considered. Areas include: the event category, genre of performers and performances, date, day, time and duration of the event; audience profile including age, the behaviour pattern of the profile, special needs, etc.; absence of seating; geography of the location and venue; topography; fire/explosion; terrorism; crowd influx and management; power failure; sudden cloud bursts, thunder and lightning, forecast of the weather, e.g. excessive heat/cold/rain; hazards on or nearby to the site, e.g. industrial plant; safety equipment failure such as CCTV and PA system; delay in start of the event, unforeseen delay or event being abandoned.

Preparation towards an incident

It is recommended to consider the following inputs while preparing a planning document for an eventuality:

- Identifying the decision-making stakeholders

- Event being abruptly stalled

- Clear plan of emergency exit, assembly points, and unhindered access for emergency services

- Plan for securing and helping guests with special needs

- Identification of safe assembly zones for performers, team, stakeholders and the team workforce;

- Details of actions to be initiated with special words to the concerned safety officials and teams

- Sounding alerts and the methodology

- Guest communication of the warnings

- Quick evacuation procedure and panic control mechanisms;

- A detailed draft of the content to be announced during an event emergency using loud speakers

- Training teams to use handheld battery-operated mics during a power outage situation.

- Identifying the points for emergency services to converge during an emergency

- Pre-determine station points for medical support teams

- The location of hospitals nearby and their capability to handle eventualities, the routes to reach and traffic diversions.

- Details of a nearby mortuary facility;

- An outline of the roles of those involved including, contact list and ways to caution and message them;

- Details of emergency equipment location and availability; documentation and emergency message boards.

f. Safety, Security and Human Factors

Emergency exit and fire fighting action list

- Has enough fire extinguishers been provided for and does it meet the safety requirements.

- Enough manpower to handle the same

- Are the right types of extinguishers located close to the fire hazards and can users gain access to them without exposing themselves to risk?

- Are the locations of the extinguishers obvious or does their position need indicating?

- Have the right teams been given the training to handle the extinguishers and are they qualified?

- Does the emergency plan include deployment of fire equipment?

- Are the exit doors warning and fire alarms regularly checked and are they in working condition?

- Are all fire doors and escape routes and associated lighting and signs regularly checked?

- Are all firefighting equipment regularly checked?

- Have all equipments meant for meeting a situation of emergency evacuation been checked

- Are those who test and maintain the equipment properly trained to do so?

- Is the fire equipment in working order and when was the last time they were checked?

- The availability of the technicians and managers for the fire equipment at the venue

- Has a demo and drill been conducted and have all concerned managers been given a printed flow chart?

- Critical to conduct a mock on the D-Day and ensure all managers part take including back-up teams

Open air venues and exit routes in an emergency situation

- Open air and outdoor venues normally have boundary fencing and these offer quick exit in an eventuality for the gathering. Identify such openings and station safety guards to enable people to use these in case of an emergency.

- Priority should be given to women with children, senior citizens and guests with special needs.

- All exits are manned by special security staff and are under their continuous watch. These are to be clearly indicated by special signs and well illuminated with visible boards.

- Right at the time of conception of an event, plan for safety aspects and involve professional safety agencies, and consult them on the safety aspects and also on managing crisis during an eventuality.

First aid

- Adequate helper staff who can offer first aid, and enough first aid apparatus need to be in place in large events and ensure the medicines used are not expired. Make sure that the basic services for first aid are always available.

- At smaller events such as indoor markets, a qualified first aid team should be available and the agency shall identify and mark a specific zone for first aid administration.

- It is also advised to hire medical service providers to offer the first aid teams to be on standby during events.

Check the following to see what the minimum for your event is

Number of people expected to attend	Number of first aid volunteers	Number of first aid posts	Ambulance
For a guest count of 500	2	1	1
For a Guest count of upto 2000	6	1	2
For a Guest count of upto 4000	8	2	2
For a Guest count of upto 5000	10	2	3
For a Guest count of upto 7000	12	3	4

- The first aid points and ambulance areas to be clearly marked and indicated.

- In events where the flying medical squads or ambulances are used, provide space close to the event to offer emergency care.

- Make announcements through sound system as also through projection on the availability of the facility at the event, and these should be repeated often.

- It is also a good practice to provide 2 phone numbers as an emergency in an event that would enable guests to connect in case of emergency.

Role of the volunteers

The duties of the volunteers are covered in detail in the appendix, here.

- The volunteers should be young and energetic teams who have prior experience or have training in handling situations.

- The number of volunteers should be in proportion to the number of guests attending the event.

- Plan the number of volunteers required based on the areas they need to cover and the number of guests they would be required to attend to in case of an emergency.

- Ensure security and health staff are located at vantage points at the venue.

- Ensure enough control is instilled across areas and activity zones.

The Art of Building Experiential Events

- Overall crowd management.

- Regular and intense patrol across event.

- Securing unauthorized zones and entry points.

- Monitoring and mapping hazards and planning managing the same.

- Car parking allocation and evacuation plan.

- The longer the event duration, the more the number of volunteers required, provide for break time and double up in emergency.

g. EHS Compliances

EHS – the most important factor in any business is relevant to event designing too. It is an abbreviation for "environment, health and safety." The EHS sets the standards, guidelines and is process oriented rule book that governs the following:

- The facility that holds an activity

- The health and safety of employees, stakeholders, visitors, guests, invitees, and the public involved in the activity

- The environment sensitivity

The purpose of the EHS guidelines can be classified as:

- Incidents that occur due to negligence and carelessness which affect the facility, environment and equipment

- Unsafe practices that directly impact and affect the people

With increased awareness levels, corporates are keen on implementing the best of safe practices and many corporate have professionally-trained teams to implement, monitor and manage EHS operations.

The best practices to be complied with under EHS guidelines include:

- All workforce at a site to work must be above the age of 18 years.

- The workforce should have on them a valid Identity card issued by the government.

- Insurance cover for the workforce is mandatory, specifying the site they are working at.

- PPEs (Personal Protection Equipment) like safety shoes, helmet, hand gloves (in case lifting of materials is there, or work with metals is involved) protective eye gear, full body double harness safety belts with double ropes are mandatory for the site workforce.

- All vehicles entering the site have to have proper and valid documents like insurance, road permits, pollution control certificate and the driver should possess valid driving license.

- The vehicle should be in good working condition and should comply with environment norms like, no oil spillage, no fuel emission beyond prescribed norms etc.

Risk assessment sheet

This has become mandatory these days across working sites for an event agency. The compliance teams need to fill in the RAS in the prescribed format of the client based on which work permits are issued.

- RAS details the work that would be executed at the site.

- The risk involved in the execution.

- The nature of risk – "normal or abnormal".

- Are electrical tools likely to be used.

- Will the execution involve working at height.

- What are the controls taken (PPE's being used.)

- Does it involve LOTO (Lock Out Tag Out)

- Are the persons who are executing the work qualified and equipped to handle the work.

- Are there any missing controls.

- Who is the site supervisor representing the client and agency.

Before the RAS is signed by the client, the following are to be completed

- Medical fitness test for the workforce will be done at site.

- EHS training will be given to all the teams.

- Temporary ID card will be issued to work at site.

- The RAS will be signed by the client and then the work permit will be issued.

Work permit

The work permit is the most important document to work in a site. Without this no material or team can enter a site, and no work can start.

- The work permit details the nature of work being executed.

- The number of people working at site.

- If work at height is involved then the necessary PPE's are checked and approved.

- Does the execution involve risky works like welding, and if so requires a special work permit?

- For electrical work LOTO needs to be done.

- The LOTO is a safety procedure done by a qualified/trained personnel from the client team.

This is to ensure that the main power switch and dangerous machines in the designated area of work is switched off to avoid mishaps.

h. Execution Plan With Complete Licensing Formalities

The table below is the grid that is evolved by the author's agency that acts as a referral document towards managing an event of this genre.

The reference document provides a holistic control dashboard in executing seamlessly. The points referred to are broad in nature and specifics are added customized to the event that is being designed.

Execution Plan with complete licensing formalities

No	Plan of action	Day – 30 to – 20	Day – 20 to – 15	Day – 15 to – 5	Day – 5 to – 2
	Promotion				
1	Paper Ad releases				
2	Paper inserts and stickers				
3	Road show promotions				
4	Ticket counter energizing				
5	Television ads/radio jingles				
6	Press conference				
	Venue readiness				
1	Recce visit to the venue				
2	Venue plan				
3	Periphery markings				

No	Plan of action	Day – 30 to – 20	Day – 20 to – 15	Day – 15 to – 5	Day – 5 to – 2
4	Entry and exit plan				
5	Safe assembly				
6	Fumigation				
7	Seating plan				
8	finalize chairs and furniture				
9	Mojo barricading finalization				
10	Genset locations				
11	Fire tender location/ambulance				
12	Site visit by authorities				

Licenses

No	Plan of action	Day – 30 to – 20	Day – 20 to – 15	Day – 15 to – 5	Day – 5 to – 2
1	Public performance license				
2	Intellectual performance rights				
3	PWD				
4	Fire and electrical department				
5	Entertainment license				
6	Safety inspection note				
7	Pollution board				

Soft Issues

No	Plan of action	Day – 30 to – 20	Day – 20 to – 15	Day – 15 to – 5	Day – 5 to – 2
1	Accommodation for celebrity				
2	Accommodation for accompanying artistes				
3	Logistics for sound and lights				
4	Security agency briefing				
5	Parking for VIP's				
6	Console mapping				
7	Filler AV designing				
8	Water counters				
9	Display stall designing				
10	Collaterals for D-Day				
11	Video and photographer briefing				

The Art of Building Experiential Events

<h2 align="center">D-Day execution plan</h2>

No	Plan of Action	Day – 1	D-Day upto noon	D-Day Event	Post D-Day
1	Security posts	▓			
2	Event ground team deployment		▓		
3	Sound and light checks	▓			
4	Emergency demo	▓			
5	Fumigation		▓		
6	Police/fire/ambulance spots			▓	
7	EHS clearance	▓	▓		
8	Safety checks	▓	▓		
9	Food and beverage for ground team		▓	▓	▓
10	Identity cards for ground teams	▓	▓	▓	▓
11	Artiste logistics	▓			
12	Vehicle allocation		▓	▓	▓
13	F&B for the performers	▓	▓	▓	▓
14	Bouncers briefing and placements	▓	▓	▓	▓
15	Exit and entry illuminated panels	▓	▓	▓	▓
16	Arch at the entrance		▓	▓	
17	Venue collaterals		▓	▓	
18	Venue illumination	▓			
19	Chairs placements	▓			
20	Mobile washrooms		▓		
21	Green room management		▓	▓	
22	Camera installation				▓
23	Talkback				▓
24	Cleaning of venue				▓
25	Exit supervisors				▓
26	Material dismantling				▓
27	Loading and departure				▓
28	Final clean-up				▓
29	Photo of the venue post clean-up				▓
30	Venue handover				▓

i. Artiste Management

The management of the celebrity/performing artiste is critical to the success of the event. Artistes, who are engaged, for such big shows, face tremendous pressure from fans, well-wishers and acquaintances. The process involved in managing the artistes is presented in an easy to map chart below.

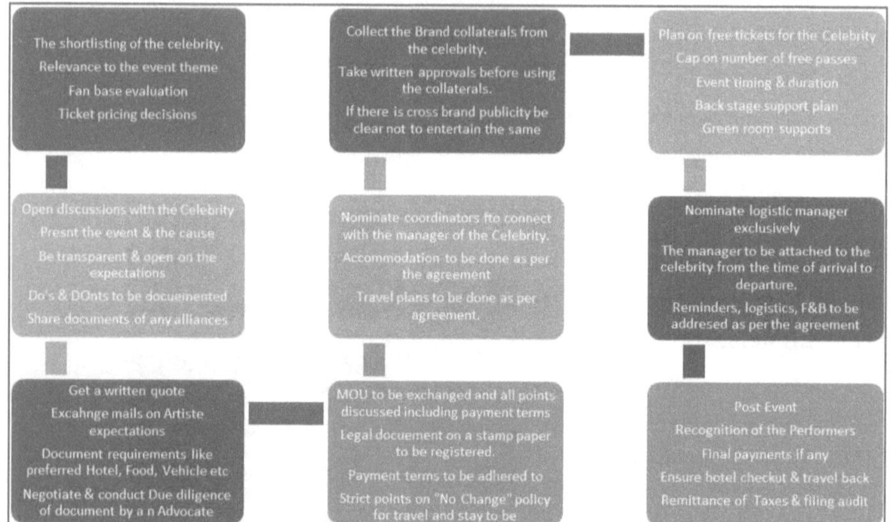

     The Art of Building Experiential Events

Chapter 11

SPECIALITY EVENTS (EXHIBITIONS AND TECHNICAL SYMPOSIUMS)

a. Sensitivity of Speciality Events

The speciality events are designed for a category/vertical of business. These events are designed for expos/technical symposiums/engineering events/sports events/ Medical Chair conferences. The sensitivities involved are very high and need an encompassed and holistic approach towards designing. The broad areas of challenges are illustrated below for quick understanding.

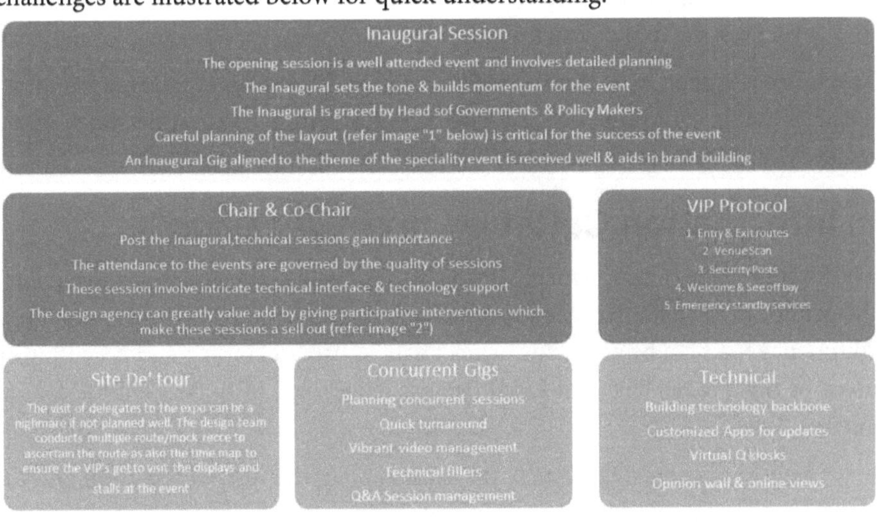

b. Sample of Non-Disclosure Agreement with the Client

While appointing an event agency, it is mandatory to sign a NDA (Non-Disclosure agreement) between the client and the design agency. Even if the client does not insist on the NDA, it is prudent for the agency to insist on signing an NDA.

The points that the NDA broadly covers are as follows:

- Transparency in communication – Communication between the 2 parties, need to be clear, straight and transparent. Any ambiguity can lead to a collapse.
- Non-disclosure of the professional fees – Professional fees paid to the partner and the deliverables are usually classified information in these type of events.
- Confidentiality with respect to using the designs developed by the agency.
- The scope of work and the objectives of the association for the purpose of the assignment.
- Guidelines on sharing of information with third parties.
- Unlawful exploitation of the association.
- Guidelines on using the brand and the logo.
- The tenure of the NDA with an information cap clause.
- Responsibility of the return of the designs used developed exclusively for the event rests with the design agency.

The NDA is signed as a moral code of conduct for the good governance of the business that is being entered into. The NDA has a time frame and validity and is reviewed at the end of the defined period to either renew or cancel it.

c. Information Collation and "Detailing"

The foremost step in commencing the designing for the speciality event is to collate the grid of the events that need to be designed and handled. The agency should commence the plan by capturing critical data towards planning and executing an event of this genre. This first input decides the course of the experience for the guests.

The grid of events, the venue, the seating plan, the time of the event and the guest count is captured as a master sheet. This sheet acts as the base document for further planning and implementation. The chart below gives a map of the said grid.

Master Document of Events

No	Event Title	Date	Time	Venue	Guest Count
1	Inauguration	20.04.16 (Saturday)	09:30 – 12:00	Convention	500-700
2	Business Conclave	20.04.16 (Saturday)	19:00 – 22:00	Hotel 1	250-300
3	Dealer Network	21.04.16 & 22.04.16	09:30 – 14:30	Convention	TBD
4	Training the Trainer	22.04.16 & 23.04.16	10:00-18:00	Convention	TBD
5	Global Network	23.04.16	10:00- 13:00	Convention	TBD
6	Gala Nite	23.04.16	19:00-22:00	Grounds	2000
7	Success through positioning	23.04.16	15:00-17:00 18:30-22:00	Convention & Lounge	TBD 250-300
8	Futurez	24.04.16	10:00-13:00	Convention	TBD

Based on the above grid, the plan of execution, allocation of resources and turn-around time is mapped. As a first step towards the execution, the perception drawing is done and shared with the client. A sample illustration of the perception drawings is shared below.

The science of designing lies in presenting to the client a visual perception of the venue layout and a detailed line drawing, is the tool for the operation team. The line drawing is the comprehensive mother document that captures the minute details of the props/inputs that go into designing the layout for the event. The planning and designing is based on the parameters listed here:

- The visibility quotient for the guests as as well as the guests of honor and the chief guest.

- The lighting and non-intrusive placement of props in the venue

- Effective placement of sound systems and their impact across the venue

- Back stage planning and props

- Support infrastructure placements and mapping

- Dais management plan and placement of furniture

- Podium, and any special requirements like floral or traditional lamp

- Placement of console and accessories

- Emergency exits and safe assembly plan

- Clearly marked aisle space at the venue and adherence to security plan

- Type and placement of seating for the guests with space for standing gallery

- Space utilization for accommodating sudden surge in guest lists

- Inputs like additional screens in the venue

The line drawing illustration below (left) details the dimensions of the venue, props, seating plan (colour coded), venue capacity, aisle space (red marking), gallery for additional guests who join for specific segments.

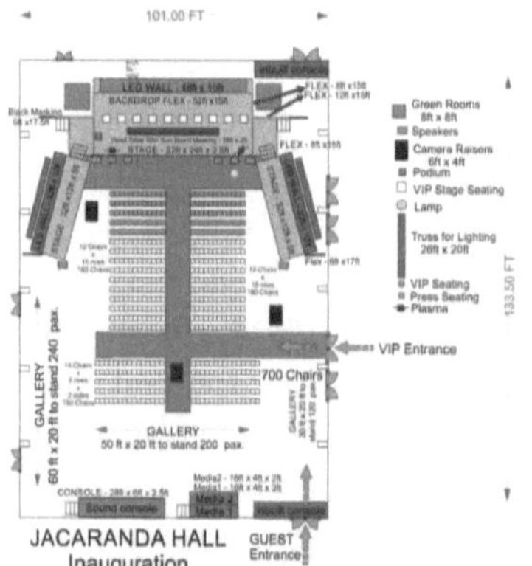

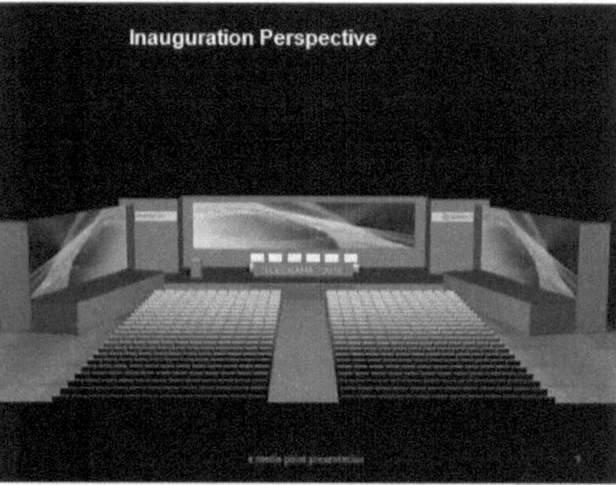

The illustration below is a sample of the master document prepared by the "client interface" team of the agency. the client interface team acts as the fulcrum with the ground team, operations team, F&B team and planning team to allocate resources, plan turn-around, ensure smooth functioning of the event, and concurrent interactions with the client for any tweaking or changes in the POA.

Days-1 to Last Day	Date	Time	Venue	Pax/Remarks
Sunday, 10th April				
Inaugural ceremony	10th April	10:00–12:00 hrs.	Blossom, convention centre,	Theatre style seating-500 – No hospitality.
VIP invitees, inaugural ceremony- For catering purpose.	10th April	09:30–12:00 hrs.	Separate area/ holding area. a) dignitaries in protocol lounge b) others in lounge	5 star hospitality – snacks – tea/coffee and cookies
Industry leaders meet	10th April	14:30 onwards	Sunflower – U shaped for 100 pax + 20 on theatre	Lunch along with delegates in the foyer
Business Summit + welcome dinner for delegates (by invitation only)	10th April	18:45–22:00 hrs.	Hotel banquets ay the city	325 pax Cluster seating- buffet + cocktails + 8 reserved tables in the front.
Monday, 11th April	**Date**	**Time**	**Venue**	**Pax/Remarks**
Business summit – inauguration	11th Apr	09:00–11:00 hrs.	Sunflower theatre style seating	300 Pax including global 50 CXOs
Chair and co-chair	11 and 12th Feb	11:30–15:00 hrs.	Sunflower – round table seating + gallery	150 Pax including global 50 CXOs – Buffet lunch at convention centre in pre-function area.
Symposium gala dinner	11th Apr Evening	19:00 hrs. onwards	Hotel banquets ay the city	250 Pax dinner, cocktails, entertainment, networking.

Days-1 to Last Day	Date	Time	Venue	Pax/Remarks
Business network	11, 12 – Full Day	10:00–17:00 hrs.	Hotel Banquets ay the city	Buffet lunch at ballroom
Tuesday 12th April	**Date**	**Time**	**Venue**	**Pax/Remarks**
Business summit	12th Apr	09:00–14:00 hrs.	Sunflower – till 1400 Hrs. – round table seating	200 Pax including global 50 CXOs – Buffet lunch at convention centre at pre-function area
Business network	11 to 15th Apr	10:00–17:00 hrs.	Hotel banquets at the city	Pl Refer – As above applicable over two and half days.
Thought leadership	11 and 12th Feb Full day	09:30–18:00 hrs.	Botanica	150 Pax – Class room style seating – Buffet 3 Star
Wednesday, 13th April	**Date**	**Time**	**Venue**	**Pax/Remarks**
Thought leadership	13th Apr	09:30–18:00 Hrs.	Botanica	150 – Class Room Style seating – buffet lunch
Global e-Business	14th Apr	10:00–16:00 hrs.	Blossom, convention centre, round table seating.	Buffet lunch at convention
Technical papers	15th Apr	10:00 Hrs.	Introduction at sunflower hall, convention centre	
TA leadership	15th Apr	11:00–15:00 Hrs.	Stall display	Assemble back at sunflower hall

The Art of Building Experiential Events

Days-1 to Last Day	Date	Time	Venue	Pax/Remarks
TA panel discussion	15th Apr	16:00–17:00 hrs.	Sunflower Hall, Convention Centre	Buffet Lunch at convention centre – tentative 150 nos as of now. – Coupons to be given
Farewell dinner	15th Apr	18:30 hrs. onwards	Open Air Auditorium	2500 Pax, Snacks, cocktail & dinner.

Credibility - is a non tangible asset that is stronger than all other qualities one may possess. More the credibility, the bigger the minds share.

– Deepak Swaminathan

Chapter 12
ANALYSIS OF AN EVENT FAILURE

a. What Is Failure (from an Event Purview)

An act of god, or an act of man which leads to a bad experience for the guests in an event can be termed as a failure. Failures directly impact the end result and events are no exception to this. Failures can be incidental or fatal. Careful planning, detailing and clear understanding of the pitfalls alone can avoid manual causes of failures.

Example of a failure

In an event designed and managed by the author's agency, there was a specific instance of failure which could have resulted in a grave situation causing tremendous damage to the brand and the event.

The failure

In a large event that had over 10000 guests for an institution's anniversary celebrations, the author's agency was the sole concessionaire for designing the event and also managing it. Though there was a clear operation grid and the process of execution was on target, the client assumed that the quantity of lights that were still being installed would be grossly inadequate for the event.

This assumption led to numerous discussions with the author and his team at the venue, even after assurances and explanations the client was unsatisfied and without informing the agency, went ahead and ordered additional dais lighting from a local vendor. As a seasoned event designer and collaborator, the author instructed his team to continue doing their work ignoring the parallel arrangement being made by the client.

The event demo session

The agency team, as is their practice, completed the set up ahead of the committed time and was ready for the demo/rehearsals. The client team was present during the demo, and simultaneously the local vendor was still doing his set up of the additional lights.

The demo session went well and the client left the venue and the agency team completed their finer tweaking and were set for the show. The local vendor was still working on putting up his additional lights as the teams were packing up post the demo, the author left back the site supervisor to ensure safety of the equipment at site.

b. How Did the Failure Happen

The event D-Day

On the D-Day the agency team completed their routine quality checks and ran yet another trial and were set for the show, and it was noticed that the local vendor hired directly by the client had put up lights on separate stands which had been fitted flouting safety standards. The local vendor had put up lights which are not event friendly and was dampening the colour hues and special effect lighting used by the author's agency.

The stability of the stand, the quality of wires, the maintenance of the lights was substandard and the efforts of the agency in convincing the client of the substandard quality fell on deaf ears. The agency operation team decided to talk it out with the local vendor advising him on the slots where he can use his lights, he appeared to be a novice on the subject of intelligent lighting, nor did he possess the state-of the-art controllers that are a definite necessity in such events.

The local vendor refused to understand the intricateness of the lighting design that was done to enhance the viewer experience. More so, he had an obsolete lighting controls, that were functioning at their own terms and the power feed was fluctuating which led to varying shades of illumination.

The incident

The event commenced and the agency team's light engineer was well-prepared and the show commenced with a specially-designed opening act with a dedication to the "supreme." This act required special lighting that would set the mood and the light engineer was completely in control of the lighting. Just at the middle of the act when the lighting hues were illuminating, the local vendor switched on his lights spoiling the experience. The first act concluded with a collusion of lighting on stage which spoiled the experience, and the client apparently realized the mistake and sent word to the local vendor to stop his illumination. *(It was too late.)*

This unplanned and unprofessional lighting on the dais at the wrong times continued in spite of repeated pleas with the local vendor both by the client and by our teams. Looking back some of the pain points caused by the wrong interventions are listed below

No	The act and type of lighting required	Wrong interventions by the local vendor
1	Opening act "salute to the energy," a combo of ochre and red illumination of dais	Bright white lights killing the brilliant act, the thought and the experience.
2	Special address by a celebrity, a spotlight illuminating the celebrity from the top and mild mix of yellow and blue to highlight the presence on the dais and black out of other areas	Super bright lights on dais to the extent of inconveniencing the celebrity that he decided to short close his speech.
3	AV being played, having erected a huge screen to play the AV means complete dimming of the dais lighting to enhance the viewer delight	As the AV was being played the light was switched on leading to unwarranted argument between the client and his new found wonder (read vendor).
4	Illusion act, special planning went into the guided lighting that was required for this act, to retain the "surprise" element. Fluorescent lights were specially installed for this experience	"Pulling the wind out of the sail" is the apt definition for the intervention done here. The illusionist act was transformed to a slapstick humour act. Thanks to the local vendor intervention.
5	Patriotic choreography, with illumination matching the color of the national flag was to have been the "scene stealer"	The local vendor stole the scene as also the image of the client.

The incident

The act of god is seen in many instances in one's life, and here we experienced it. During one of the unplanned interventions by the local vendor, there were sudden fumes that came from the lights and it was from the poor quality of wires that were burning. The wires were not suited for the load of the lights, and the vendor who was unaware of the science behind the load calculation was still justifying that it would be alright in a while.

Our experienced team of technicians were quick to sense the impending danger and were quick to act. The alertness of our team by quickly pouring sand on the wire and forcefully switching off the main board that supplied the power helped in saving from the worst happening.

This "calamity" helped us overcome this "unplanned intervention" and to turn the rest of the event into a cherished and memorable experience for the client and for their guests. The client was made aware of the folly and had some kind words of support for us.

c. The Client-Agency Deliberation Mapping of the Failure

Post the event there were event audit discussions with the client and the following were the points that were taken for the evaluations.

No	Points addressed	Feedback from the client	Reasons
1	The fabrication with special focus on branding themes	Excellent	
2	The back stage management of mementoes/gifts	Good	Managed by the client teams with agency facilitation
3	Sound quality at the venue (open air)	Excellent	
4	Lighting and special effects	Average	External intervention
5	Projection and delay projection and content management	Excellent	
6	Celebrity management	Good/Celebrity complained of the food served	Complaint on the quality of F&B served
7	F&B partner selection	Poor	Was selected by the client and agency had limited role to play
8	Security and safety management	Excellent	
9	Program management	Excellent	

 The Art of Building Experiential Events

No	Points addressed	Feedback from the client	Reasons
10	Turnover of program sequences	Excellent	
11	Media management	Excellent	
12	Overall rating from client	Good	

d. The Identification of the Cause of the Failure

No	The area of failure (in order of priority)	The cause and effect	The learning
1	Lighting	Unplanned intervention using substandard lighting team caused havoc in the event. The quality of lights, non-clarity on the usage, non-alignment to the event brief, non-understanding of the finesse led to a bad experience, and could have turned into a dangerous one too.	Ensure the customer is well-educated on the process of "work at site" and clearly mark the timelines for client intervention.
2	F&B Partner	Selection of F&B partner has a process and the agency though offered choices of tried and tested F&B partners, the client was keen on their choice.	Have an MOU on the roles and Responsibilities of the agency and be forthright on the views of the agency with regard to selection of key partners like the F&B, security, paramedics etc.
3	Back stage management	Altering the agenda mid-way to the whims and fancy of the client can cause confusion in the back stage leading to disruption in the proceedings like giving away mementoes etc.	Insist on one "contact point" for back stage support for any changes or decisions. Invariably multiple instructions are the cause of such anomalies.

e. The Back-Up Plan That Was in Place

In this case study, the back-up plan that was in place to face this eventuality is given below, the grid is a step-by step action that was planned and implemented by the agency which turned out to be the saviour.

No	Identification of the friction point	Action initiated
1	Doubt raised by the client on the lighting impact during the setting up.	During the setting up time, any client who walks in will have their doubts as the site where the work is in progress will not resemble the final venue. On identification of this point, the agency team discussed internally and implemented the following: • The standby stock of special effect lighting was also fitted to the truss. • Advanced the demo time and ensured the light engineer was available through and after the demo for any tweaking.
2	When the client decided to call in a local vendor to provide additional lighting.	The agency team tried their best to deliberate with the client explaining that the additional lighting will not be required, but the client was not in agreement. Sensing this, the agency went ahead and • Allocated resource at site to check the quality of lights • Ensured no connections were shared between the 2 vendors • Strategically placed the agency lighting sensors away from the local vendors points • Took snaps of the quality of stands, lights and connections that were being done by the local vendor • Dedicated one personnel for quality check of the local vendor's lighting
3	During the event and when the disruption took place.	The agency team, prior to the event commencement, posted one personnel at the console of the local light vendor, who was constantly monitoring and urging the light vendor to allow our person to operate on the equipment.

No	Identification of the friction point	Action initiated
		Our team was also alert as the quality person had forewarned about the substandard equipment that were being used. Hence the briefing to our person was as follows • Befriend the vendor and try to operate the controls so that the effect of the main lighting will not be affected. • Watch out for any issues like short circuit, fire, etc. and be quick to act. • Our safety person and a security guard were posted near the local vendor's console and as expected there was a disruption and the timely intervention by the team prevented a calamity.

f. Analysis of Preventing Such Failures from Occurring

The learning from this failure helped the agency to fix few more areas which are listed below. These points helped in improving the interface and understanding the clients and also helped in improving the quality of solutions that we delivered.

- Involve light and sound engineers to explain the process involved in designing and setting up.

- Instruct clients not to come to site during the set up or give a time for client visit and demo.

- Quality checks to be run with the client by the agency quality team to educate on the importance QC.

- Operation flow presentation to be a mandatory protocol and take the concurrence of the client at stages.

- On selection of partners, wherever the agency is not involved, it is wise to stay away from all decision, however educate the client on the pitfalls and the shortcomings.

- Event flow document to be shared with the client capturing all factors end-to-end and summarise the roles and responsibilities of all stakeholders with clear deliverables and also penalty if any for the shortcoming.

- A well-established agency should challenge the client during the discussion sessions on the points that can bring in frictions and provide solutions that are viable, acceptable and implementable.

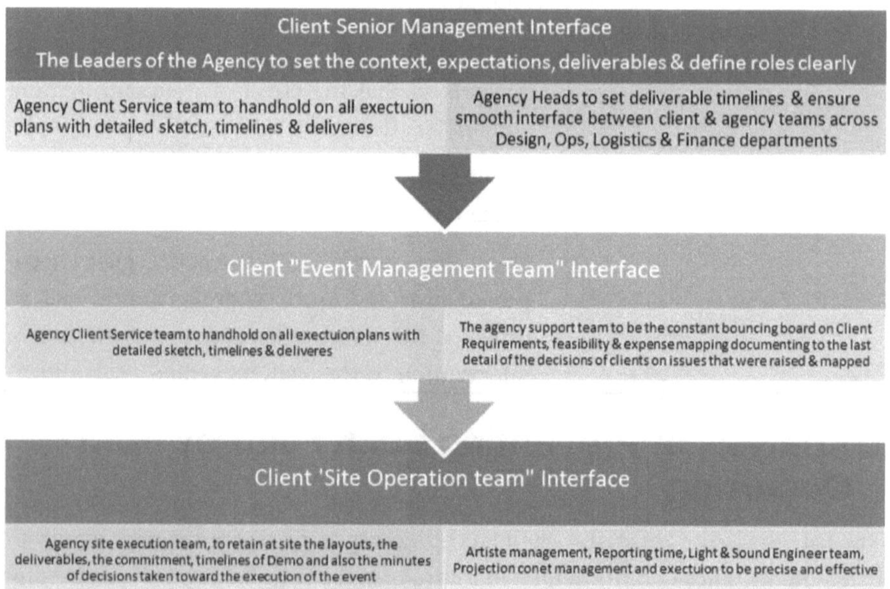

The following grid details 3 segments which needs the "right" inputs to ensure the "correct" planing of the event. Out of experience it is noticed that if these 3 areas are focussed the assignment is well executed. More often as we move closer to the event date, many new guests from the client side get involved and in most cases this leads to tremendous delivery issues for the agency thus spoiling the event experience. The best way an event can be handled is through process-oriented documentation." Mapping every step, focus on challenging areas, identifying the failure zones and escalating and concurrent addressing of issues are the secrets to success in designing and managing events.

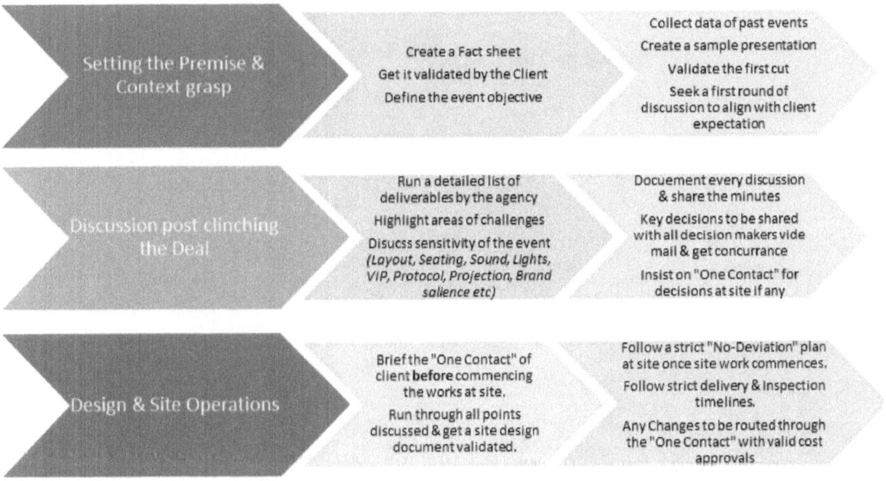

Setting the Premise & Context grasp

- Create a Fact sheet
- Get it validated by the Client
- Define the event objective
- Collect data of past events
- Create a sample presentation
- Validate the first cut
- Seek a first round of discussion to align with client expectation

Discussion post clinching the Deal

- Run a detailed list of deliverables by the agency
- Highlight areas of challenges
- Disucss sensitivity of the event *(Layout, Seating, Sound, Lights, VIP, Protocol, Projection, Brand salience etc)*
- Docuement every discussion & share the minutes
- Key decisions to be shared with all decision makers vide mail & get concurrance
- Insist on "One Contact" for decisions at site if any

Design & Site Operations

- Brief the "One Contact" of client **before** commencing the works at site.
- Run through all points discussed & get a site design document validated.
- Follow a strict "No-Deviation" plan at site once site work commences.
- Follow strict delivery & Inspection timelines.
- Any Changes to be routed through the "One Contact" with valid cost approvals

If we are not able to deliver a promise, so be it. But not having the grit &
courage to face it defines the quantum of success that's in store.

– Deepak Swaminathan

Chapter 13

REASONS WHY AN EVENT FAILS

Events can fail for a variety of reasons and this business is so volatile that there are too many external factors which can play havoc, however with accurate planning and rich experience the challenge areas can be addressed to enhance the "wow" experience of an event.

Presented below is a broad overview of areas which can cause an event to fail.

a. Mismatch Between Promises and Reality

No	Activity that can be the cause of "Failure"	Pain point
1	Client servicing	Setting high expectations on deliverables
		Over commitment to win a client and to meet a target
		Exposing the inherent weakness of a team or a member
		Avoiding client calls post a confirmation
		Providing false information
		Not keeping up delivery deadlines
		Not understanding the requirements in full
		Miscommunication internally
2	Designing team	Thrusting a design that a client is not inclined to
		Communication gap within the agency that leads to wrong designing
		Being unprepared for the designing meeting with the client
		Informing clients that other client works are keeping them busy
		Not meeting deadlines as committed

No	Activity that can be the cause of "Failure"	Pain point
		Not incorporating certain key elements that are critical
		Non-focus on the assignment leading to substandard designs
		Non-compliance to brand identity
3	Finance planning	Preparation of wrongly worded MOU
		Insufficient document submission
		Not completing empanelment formalities within defined time frame
		Submission of invoice with errors
		Non-compliance in empanelment
		Poor support documentation
		False information or misrepresentation
4	Logistic team	Incomplete master sheet of priority pick up and categorization of guests
		Poorly trained manpower at the logistic point
		Errors in planning and execution of logistics
		Improper briefing to drivers and welcome teams
		Insensitivity of the check-in support
5	Operations team	Delay in arrival of props to the venue
		Deviation from delivery deadlines at site
		Miscommunication of timelines
		Unpreparedness for contingency
		License and permissions issues
		Delay in handover for demo
		Weak reasons behind delays or non-deliverables
		Non-escalation of critical issues
6	Ground and console management team	Artistes and performers briefing and reporting
		Backstage marksman for coordination
		Console management

No	Activity that can be the cause of "Failure"	Pain point
7	Post event support team	LED content management
		Sound, lights technical management
		Cue sheet briefing and linear mapping
		Technical back-up management at the console (power, cables etc.)
		Delay in handing over of client props
		Short delivery in photography
		Error in video edits
		Ensuring all client videos are deleted from the agency servers
		Compliance towards dismantling and reporting post an event
		Cleaning venue and handover

b. Customer Oversight

In reality the success of an event is attached to the client and the failure to the design agency. Hence it is for the event design agency to have complete control on all aspects of the event. The success of an event invariably ensures "loyalty" for the agency and assured recurring business and referrals. The following are some areas where the customer misses out on the briefing out of oversight or out of ignorance.

No	Failure point caused due to client	Agency hand hold
1	During the first Briefing Missing out on some points Non-availability of some inputs at the time of meeting	Share a brief document capturing all points discussed and get it validated via e-mail Run all the points and remind them for inputs that were to be shared at a later date
2	Bouquet, photographer and video briefing Protocol document of VIP visits	The Bouquet/floral, photo and video is always given a miss, hence include in the initial discussions. Protocol document is another mandate which is sensitive in nature.

No	Failure point caused due to client	Agency hand hold
		The agency team need to encompass the docket requirements into their designing
3	The welcome point for chief guest and VIPs	Till the D-Day this decision is kept in abeyance. The welcome point designated for the Chief guest has to be decked up and this required time. A professional agency plans ahead and proposes 2 locations for the welcome and customizes the welcome deck in a way that it is light, sturdy yet easy to move and re-fix. This will help avoid complex situations if a decision is changed at the last minute
4	Gifts/mementoes for the guest of honour and chief guest	Putting a process in place and educating a client in handling this prevents embarrassment of mixing the mementoes. Colour coded mementoes and scanner readers are options to ensure that the right memento is handed over. Collecting the memento for safe keeping and handling by the agency is right process
5	Essentials ambulance/paramedics	Agency scope includes safety, and hence Ambulance/paramedics is a MUST
	limited knowledge or no knowledge in permissions	License and permissions are usually left out as the client is ignorant of the rules. It is the responsibility of the agency team to educate, procure and manage the permissions

The Art of Building Experiential Events

c. Cost Cutting

There is a perennial gap between arriving at the balance between the expectations of a client vs. spends for an activity. The initial briefing from a client sets high expectations, and benchmarks, however this expectation is an "ideal experience" and in reality the budgets make a difference in matching the expectations.

With a wide experience the author has mapped following as the areas where costs cannot be curtailed as this will impact the experience. If the client is a regular, then the agency will enjoy a special relationship in which case the agency will be able to use their expertise and decide on behalf of the client.

No	Area of focus
1	**Venue:**
	No compromise on the venue shall be entertained as this forms the "foundation" to design the event. Venue selection is based on various criteria as discussed earlier in the document. A compromise in the venue will impact the event.
2	**Sound, lights and power:**
	Half the experience is defined by the quality of interactivity in an event. Having mentioned that, the quality of sound, the placements, the audibility, the comfort and the visual colourful appeal caused by the lights and ensuring uninterrupted power makes the event memorable and enjoyable. It is the basic duty of the event team to ensure this area is not compromised at all as a bad sound and poor illumination will drive away the audience.
3	**Projections and content management:**
	With the advent of online platforms guests are exposed to an array of content at the comfort of their phone and at their homes. The design agency, needs to innovate on a continuous basis to retain the eye balls for an event. Technically providing the right solution for a projection and effective content management with intelligent inputs alone can ensure recall of an event. This is yet another area where costs cannot be curtailed
4	**Safety and Security:**
	This area is a strict "no compromise" aspect and the author has mapped this adequately in the earlier section. Planning sufficient safety managers, security commensurate to the category of the event and safe assembly points are mandatory and cannot be compromised.

d. Client vs. Agency Iteration Mismatch

The agency and the client need to align their thinking and exchanges to the common objective without which the association will be a non-starter. With a wide experience of working on pan event genres, the points referred here are areas where the mismatch in iteration can cause the association to collapse and result in losing the assignment.

- Setting the context and the expectation mapping
- Ignorant to the subtle cues raised by the clients with regard to costs
- Agency not realizing the core issues that need solutions
- Agency reinforcing the "We know what will work" attitude
- Branding designs which go against the corporate identity norms
- Insensitivity to the "protocol requirements"
- Improper planning and poor designing
- Non-process oriented approach
- Communication issues between client coordinators and agency coordinators
- Flouting safety norms
- Hiding of facts and wrong representations
- Missing out on critical data that is required for planning
- Deviation of NDA
- Non-submission of empanelment documents
- Reopening estimate discussions post decision
- Over commitment on deliveries and ending up in short deliveries
- Corporate brand compliances
- Incompetent personnel
- Substandard quality of solutions
- Repetitive and uninteresting design solutions
- Negative market feedback

Our clients come to us in search of expertise, share it with them, show that you care, the results may not immediately warm up but the flavour of your warm style will result in sustained relationship & wonderful business collaboration.

– Deepak Swaminathan

Chapter 14
TOOLS FOR MEASURING EVENT DESIGNING

a. 6 Ways to Measure Success of an Event

Social Media Networking
1. Monitor registrations
2. Useful Engagement with prospects
3. Incentives for visiting
4. Response from visitors
5. Post event flavour

Post Event Analysis
1. Core group connect programs
2. E-reviews & opinion polls
3. Visitor delight mapping
4. Direct feedback collection

Revenue Vs Expenditure
1. Actual Vs Estimated cost
2. Attendees Vs Estimates
3. Good Vs Average feedback
4. Value proposition in attending

Sponsor Recognition
1. Order Booking at the event
2. Feedback of Clients' Client
3. Points of criticism by sponsor
4. Online posting of event

Post Event Audit
1. Number of Negatives on delivery
2. Customer satisfaction survey
3. Intent to re-appoint the agency
4. Reference & Video bytes

Incorporate an Event App
Include their event schedule or agenda in the app for staffers and attendees to view
Allow guests to personalize their own schedules and set reminders
Allow guests to post comments and feedback for event planners and guest speakers
Store, scan, and exchange digital business cards
Embed company and sponsor banners
Send announcements in real time, such as changes in schedule or parking space availability

b. Grid for Objective Evaluation

With the advent of professional agencies and capable evaluating teams, events have to move towards meeting set objectives. Every assignment needs to be measured for its results from which stems further changes for betterment. In the parlance of a business these can be defined as Return on the Investment, however in events this term may not directly represent monetary values, however returns intangible values and benefits.

Objective Evaluation Methodology

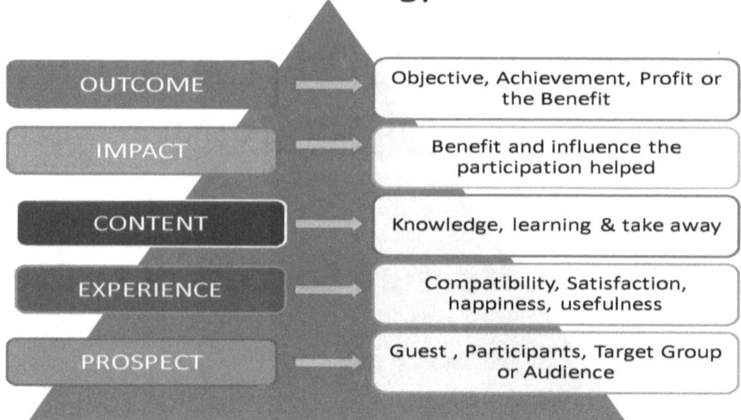

With the experience of close to 2 decades, the author, who had started as a small event handling agent, moved up the value chain and set up an organization that is completely process driven with a team of capable and well qualified professionals. The progressive growth came in when the events were measured for their objectives and successes. Once the focus is set on a specific objective, drawing up plans which will help reach this goal is not difficult. A systematic approach, meticulous planning and an all-encompassing intervention across levels of designing events is a sure shot winner which aptly satisfies the objective.

Each event has a different objective. The table below shows the possible objectives of events which will further the understanding.

No	Event Genre	Objective
1	Sales Meet & Annual Conference	• Recognizing teams • Motivation • Target setting for the upcoming year • Commitments and assurances
2	Awards Nite	• Brand Building • Premium image for the Award • Visibility & Recognition
3	Government Event	• People Welfare • Art & Culture • Visibility for Scheme s
4	Product Launch	• Dealer attendance • On spot feedback • Bookings • Brand Building
5	Medical Conferences	• Technical sessions • New Formulations • Popularity amongst fraternity • Netwroking

The Art of Building Experiential Events

Outcome

The outcome, achievement or benefit is the desired result one expects from conducting an event. This decides the fate of the event and its continuity. Many a time clients decide on sustaining their association with the agency based on the outcome of an event.

Impact

How do the guests benefit by attending an event? Have they seen value in association? What have been special features that have made the event valuable for the participant? The inference of each participant may well be different as the expectations would have been different too. Few actions may be critical (e.g. order bookings in a dealer meet) whereas others only make a smaller impact to the outcome, like increasing the chances of a purchase in a demo event (e.g. ask for more information, share knowledge with colleagues, seeking alternatives etc.). There can be a shift in the buying pattern post attending an event, a positive change in the involvement of a purchase.

Content

What holistic change can be brought in to the experience at an event is decided by the content. The more interesting the content, and the more involving the experience the more the participation of the guest in an event. The content if made interesting, can bring about a cognitive change. The change can be so intrinsic that it can alter the behaviour of the buyer.

Experience

How can the environment be made memorable? By giving the right experience. That experience will make an effective cognitive change. Experience infuses learning and can become a permanent installation leading to a positive change. Our guests are the most important reason for us to be in the business of designing events, and it is imperative to adhere to building experiences that will benefit not only the sponsor but also our valued guests. Apart from the ambience, high quality audio systems, experience is also highly derived from the quality of presentations, the quality of delegates and more importantly the quality of speakers who make the experience memorable and involving.

Prospect

The most fundamental part of an event is the prospect. Choosing the right prospect, decides the final fibre of an event. There can be a few check points that can aid in deciding and fixing on the prospect for an event, the profile, the benefit they would derive, their expectations, current market realities, the usefulness of the promotion or an event to the prospect, the peer groups and the influencer group expectations. Once these points are clearly defined and mapped, the identification, with the prospect will be an easy task.

Measure matrix

The objective evaluation methodology can further be analysed using the Measure Matrix, which helps in arriving at the desired level of success. The Measure Matrix is penetration model that commences with the first level which is the guest or target and it reached the core which is "outcome." Each level is measured scientifically, can help understand a behaviour pattern that can be harnessed in defining the fibre of an event.

Measure Matrix

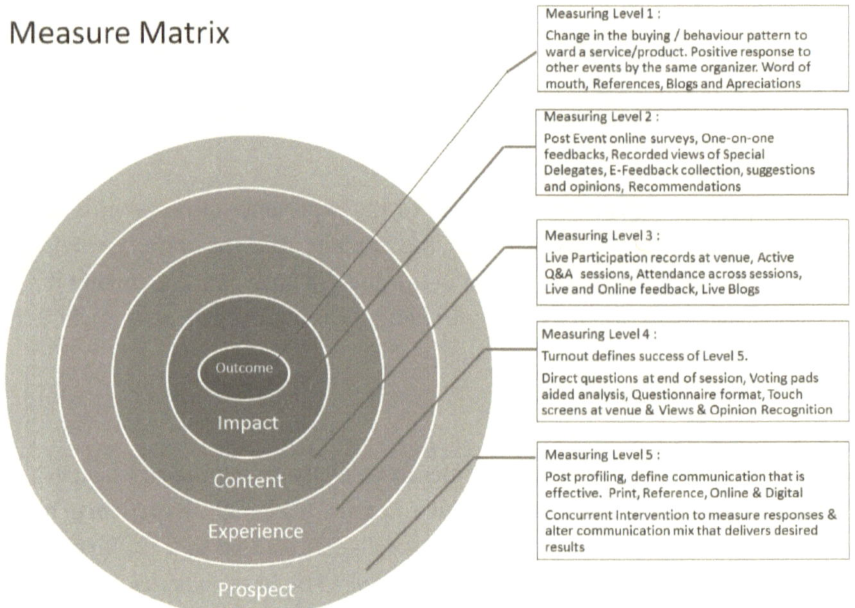

The "Objective Meeting" exercise

In a typical case of evaluating or measuring a success of an event, the illustration here can help understand and affirm if the desired objective is met or not.

For example, if it is a customer event for a product demo and sale, and post the event if the sale had gone up, does it necessarily mean that the event was the reason for the sale to go north? To understand this better, it is imperative to isolate target group. Categorize people as follows:

 The Art of Building Experiential Events

- Group who attended the event alone
- Groups who attended the event and were exposed to ads
- Groups who did not attend the event

Once the categorization is complete, then applying sales to the groups as classified above will give a clear input on the effect of the event. There can also be contradicting results between the groups. The group which attended an event and if the sales, has indeed been effective, then it's a fair conclusion to draw that the product has been well-received.

Another method adopted is the controlled group experience. Here the agency works extensively at the ground level and invites prospects that are technically aware of a development, however do not possess knowledge on the product or its uses. This effort, involves in bringing the defined prospect, to a specific event experience and the groups is allowed to experiment, discuss and dwell on the product. The outcome will be reliable and can be best used for furthering campaign. This method is expensive and resource consuming, and is ideal for products that are high priced and technically advanced.

Equating outcome to profit

Some events can be directly equated to profit based on sales or invoicing. However there are many categories that cannot be directly equated to profit or inflow, however if the set objective is met, then those are classified as profitable or objective attained events. An event for the human resource department may lead to reduced attrition or improved efficiency, and here the motive is achieved and the outcome is successful.

In an annual sales conference, the "outcome" is in getting a firm commitment of the target for the coming year, increase in the morale of the team and achievement of targets as was mapped in the earlier conference and increase in market presence.

Conclusion

Events and conferences have also become an important quotient in the planner's scheme of things. From being an unorganized system, MICE (Meetings, Incentives, Conferencing and Exhibitions) have become an integral part. The expenses on this head may look controllable, but the intangible values and far reaching benefits in the minds of audience make this category unavoidable. If the agency comes about as a true partner that weighs "objectivity" over just execution, that agency stands to gain phenomenal ground in the business of event designing and execution.

c. An Effective Event Designing Process Tool

Surveys are indispensable event planning tools, when used correctly. They can help that your event is a success by enabling you to gauge expectations, understand participant reaction during the event, and measure the effectiveness of your message, after the event is over. Online survey tools enable you to gather and analyse information before, during, and after an event—in a fast, effective, and affordable manner.

Matrix of Evaluation

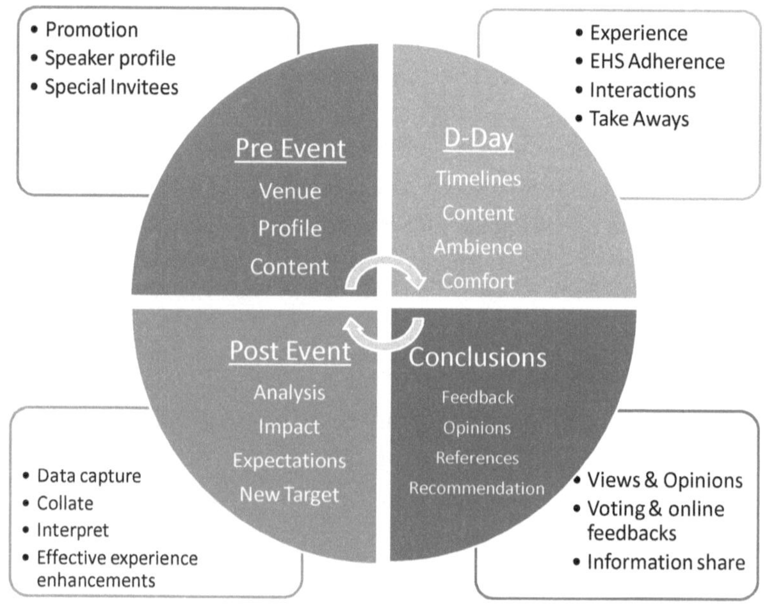

The Art of Building Experiential Events

Its good to work hard, its a pleasure to see smiles, its great to win challenges, but more than all..its important to keep working SMART with consistency.

– Deepak Swaminathan

Chapter 15

VENDOR-PARTNER MANAGEMENT

The best of successes in this world is achieved not just by the hard work of one person or team, behind the success lies the unspelt efforts of partners/vendors and many unsung heroes. The world of information technology wouldn't have been a stupendous success but for the numerous vendor partners across the value chain.

So it's critical not only that you have collegial relationships with your event vendors but that you also manage them properly to ensure they meet your expectations and those of your clients. Here are a few things to keep in mind when keeping track of them:

a. Identifying and Grooming a Vendor Partner

As in every trade vendor partners play a vital role in designing and executing an event. The selection of a vendor is not an easy process as it is a combination of belief, ethics, passion and professional competence.

The identification of a vendor is governed by the following parameters:

- Industry reference (a minimum of 2 references on capability and delivery).
- Existence in the field (number of years).
- Presence across zones.
- Capability of the teams of the vendor.
- Registration with the authorities.
- Supporting documents of the sphere of events associated with.

Once the vendor shortlist is done as per the above criteria, follow a format for grooming and empanelling the vendor partner, the steps involved in grooming and empanelling is specified below:

- Vendor to submit a detailed presentation of their capabilities.
- Visit to the vendor office/warehouse to evaluate and validate their capability submissions.
- An MOU with non-disclosure points, special tariff arrangements, payment terms and priority rating.

- Demo, trials and testing sessions.

- EHS compliances, safety at work and induction program.

- Signing of an annual rate card categorizing the genre of services to be rendered.

- Work at site manual detailing do's and don'ts

b. Empanelment Process

The empanelment process is in itself a relationship building exercise, wherein the vendor partner appreciates the commitment of the client (read agency) in commencing and nurturing a relationship, this process is critical from the view point of supporting in delivering to the expectations as also inking a firm association between the 2 parties.

The process of empanelment is done with the completion of the formalities listed herein:

- A letter from the banker endorsing the business account

- Details of their financial capabilities

- Copy of the business registration certificate

- Tax registration documents

- Business reference forms

- Bank details, a cancelled cheque leaf

- Government registration numbers authorized by their bankers

On collection of the above documents, a draft agreement with the understanding is done and both parties sign it as a mark of acceptance. The said document specifies the validity of the contents and the association will be reviewed from time to time with changes as warranted by the business.

c. Six Steps in Improving Vendor Management

It's critical not only that you have collegial relationships with your event vendors but that you also manage them properly to ensure they meet your expectations and those of your clients. Here are a few things to keep in mind when keeping track of them:

- Document and discuss you expectations and exchange the same in paper

- Have a separate contract for each project

- Share detailed layouts, developments and define expectations for each activity

   The Art of Building Experiential Events

- Clearly specify delivery deadlines

- Double check your orders with the deliveries for accuracy

- Ensure fair negotiation and operate on a "win-win situation"

d. Best Practice in Vendor Management

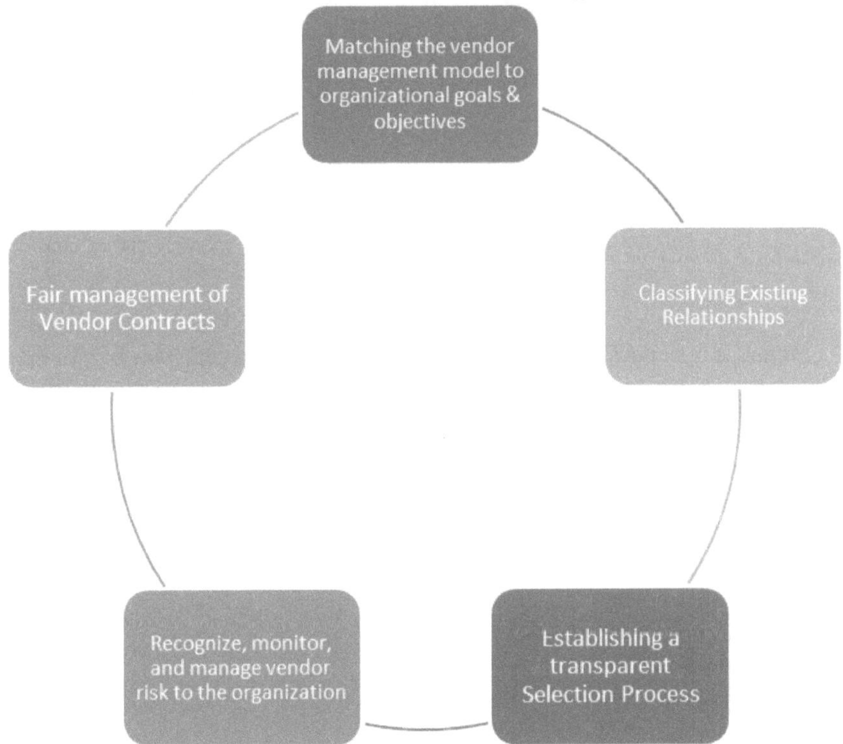

Failure is a beautiful experience... The dawning of hope, the innate efforts, renewed thinking forms the canvas for sketching success.

– Deepak Swaminathan

Chapter 16

CLARION

The business of "experiential" events is like treading on a slippery ground, what seems to be a great idea at the discussion room can turn out to be the most uninteresting experience at site, and what seems like a not so exiting idea can pan out to be the most celebrated one. The essence lies in getting under the skin of our client and their clients, and viewing the idea from the eye of a critique. The more the disruption to the idea the more is the "experience quotient."

The business of events is highly strenuous and exhaustive, and is aptly defined by the term "events." These are one time acts and there are, no retakes and redefining. All innovations have to be pre-mapped, tried and tested, at the same time the ability to be prepared to face a crisis and the grit to handle the same without disrupting the event is the biggest challenge.

This illustration substantiates the challenging genre of the event management business. The expectations can be well defined, the solutions can be discussed at length, the challenges can be drawn out too, but unless the team possess a passion to the craft, delivering "intelligent and strategic" events is impossible. The Career Cast 2016 Job stress report, classifies this trade under the 5 most stressful careers; however the returns are not commensurate to the status it enjoys among the other 4 Jobs.

The ideal components that need to feature in the pitch of a successful agency as designed by the author is shared below. With wide experience in multi-genre events, and with no formal education support for the category of "experiential events," the learning from each event, constant upgrading of knowledge, keeping pace with newer technologies, innovative application of the available resources and finally the capability to visually map the event from an "audience's" perspective coupled with comprehensive understanding of the challenges alone aids in designing and delivering "experiential events."

The Essentials of "Value-Based Business Conduct"

Like in any field of business, events are an intrinsic part of the marketing and promotion pie of a brand. Events are the windows of opportunities that connect the end user with the product or solution. For an organization in the business of event designing to succeed, the vision need to be long-term, the investments of resources need to be continuous, and evolution sustained.

The author with a wide exposure of having executed on a "first-hand basis" over 4000 events leads by example of high values and ethical business conduct. By adopting stringent policies of values and ethics, the business has evolved from being a one city agency to being an agency with a pan India presence with numerous branches overseas panning Middle East to East Asia.

The success of an agency lies in the ability to deliver exceeding the expectations of the client yet remaining a preferred partner for the client/brand. The author's agency takes pride in every relationship that were commenced and have been sustaining with a success rate of about 90%. The most satisfying of the experiences was being nominated as a sole concessionaire for about 10 leading clients with whom we had shared a relationship of over a decade.

Presented below is a reference chart of the most critical components in building a "value-based" system which if nurtured with great care and passion, will result in a firm bonding with clients leading to numerous opportunities.

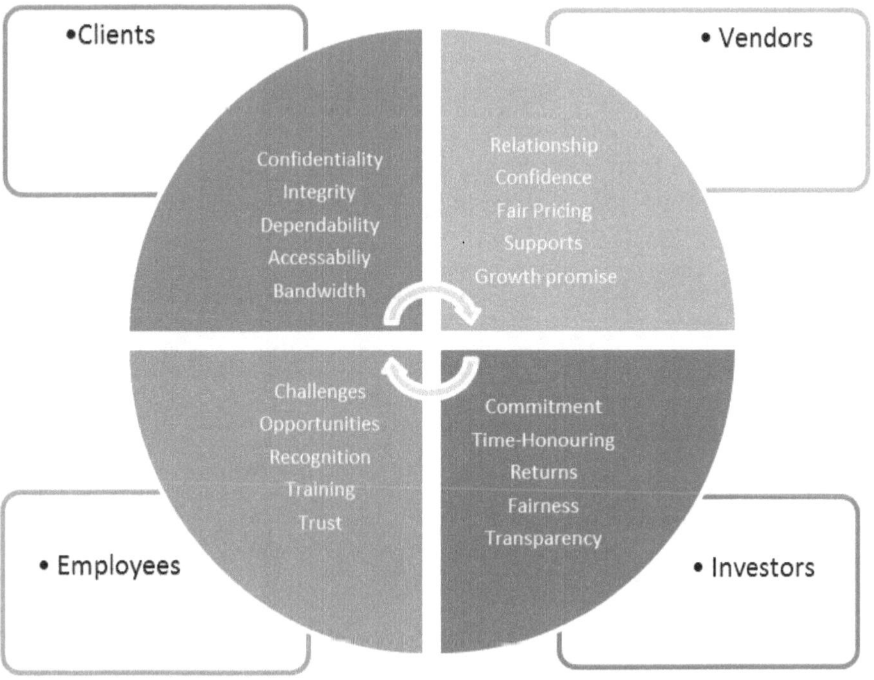

The value is a chain of commitment to the external and internal stakeholders of the business, any deviation in the values and beliefs disturbs the eco system thus spoiling the balance and harmony. The values are equal to growing a tree and like a tree it needs tremendous investment of thoughts, deed and action to consistently and continuously demonstrate the commitment at every opportunity.

Each component in the above grid are like spokes in a strong wheel, any imbalance to one of them leads to chaos and derailment of the system. The author believes in equal recognition and strives to deliver superior experiences to each of the above partners thus building an edifice of "value-based business conduct."

Author compiled graph of "Experiential Events"

Finding an optimum point in an experential event is a challenge and sustaining the optimum point is the "biggest achievement" in the business. The experience of having worked with varied category of brands and clients has taught numerous lessons in the business of designing experential events.

The author has put together a "self taught" model fused with rich experience drawn from the wide spectrum of events that have been designed by his organizarion under his leadership. The said graph is illustrated below and has evolved over time and events. The graph has the 'x' axis which is the "experience quotient" i. e the representation of the level of "experience" at the event for the guests. The 'y' axis is the expense for the event and here the axis flows from the top to the bottom where the expense grows from least expensive to most expensive. The graph attempts to plot the ideal event situation that brings in the maximum "experience" for the guests at an optimal spending level.

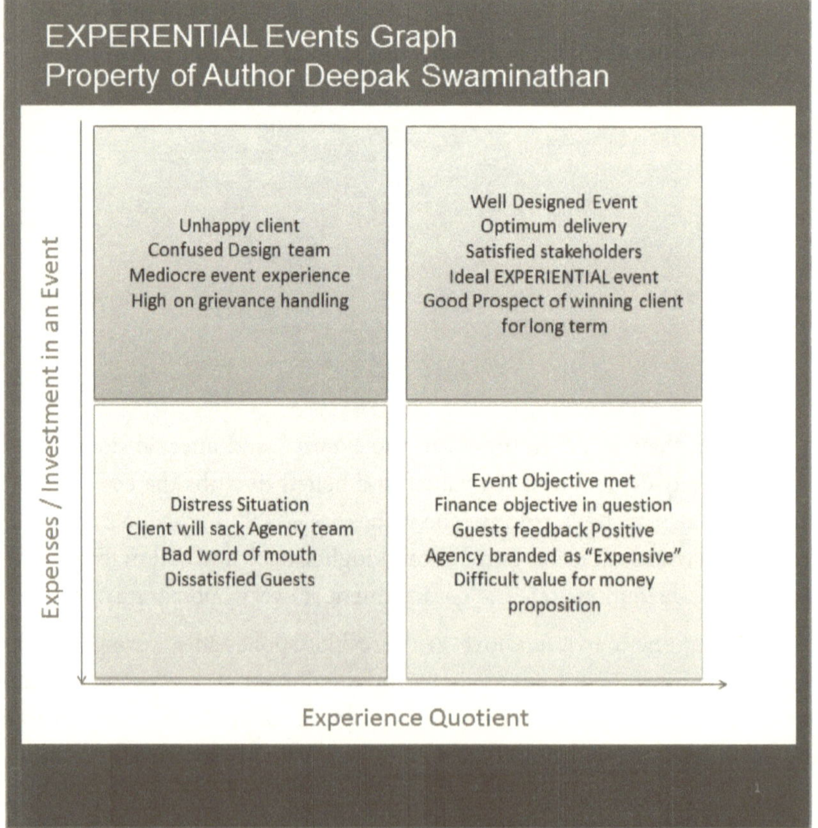

 The Art of Building Experiential Events

An ideal situation is marked in "red" which is the preferred point that balances the "expense or investment with the best of experience" this point is called as the "most preferred slot" wherein the objectives of the Investor (client) and the agency align delivering the best of an "experience" with the right deployment of resources with the right quantum of investment.

The right experience also opens up an opportunity in getting the preferred partner status with the client. More often, the client looks up to the agency for arriving at the "optimum point" and if the agency team is quick to sense this expectation, can build up on the same by offering solutions to the challenges in all areas concerning the event and thereby strengthening the ties between the client and the agency.

The eco system

The eco system balance is critical to the effective functioning of the business model, for the best development of the business both for players and the market to grow, a healthy eco system is essential. Presented below is the "Eco System" concerning the "experience event" category.

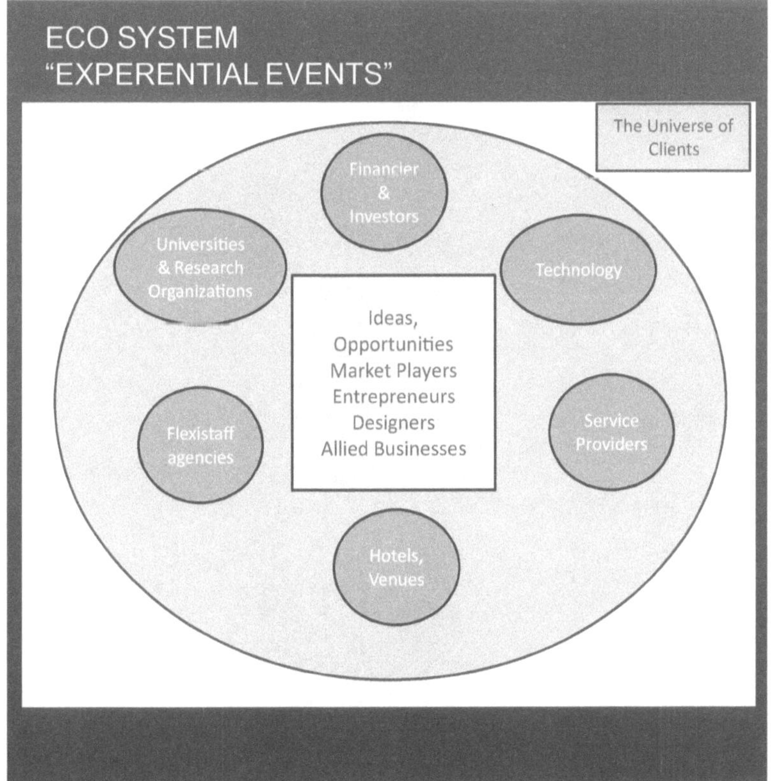

Conclusion

The opportunities are abundant and the business domains are infinite. The most innate thing that remains constant in the "experential event" is the "experience," the fibre, the elements. The source codes keep varying and are dynamic. The world is fast moving from providing -> *customising*; from availability -> *convenience*; from delivery -> *designing your experience*—thus the art of experiential events. This process of providing, availability and delivery are the hardware, while the process of customising, convenience and designing your experience are the software of a good event system. The changes and the dynamic nature of the software determine the nature of the hardware.

In pursuit of superior experiences the sub eco system of the bsuiness revolves dynamically by offering unique, cost effetive and sustainable solutions which ushers in a whole new world of "experientially desirable events."

With a memorable past and a promising tomorrow, let's cherish every moment at hand to make events "memorable and special."

Client Credits

1. ALSTOM T&D India Ltd.
2. ALSTOM Transport India Ltd.
3. Apollo Paints Pvt Ltd.
4. Fulcrum Venture India
5. Honeywell Technology Solutions
6. Indian Electrical & Electronics Manufacturers Association (IEEMA)
7. Mahindra World City – (Mahindra Life space Developers Ltd.)
8. Parker Hannifin India Pvt Ltd.
9. Shield Healthcare Pvt Ltd.

Special Thanks

1. *Pt BickramGhosh – Percussionist*
2. *Shri Vishal & Shri Sekhar – Composers*

My Sincere Thanks

- *Shri Srinivasan K Swamy – Chairman & Managing Director R K Swamy BBDO Private Limited*
- *Dr. R.Lakshmipathy – Publisher – Dinamalar*
- *Shri Sunil Misra – Director General* – Indian Electrical & Electronics Manufacturers Association (IEEMA)
- *Shri Rajiv Menon- Director, Cinematographer, Writer*

This book is a reality, thanks to the wonderful support of my family who have been my strength applauding every milestone.

Special Thanks to my colleagues who have stood by me in delivering 4000+ events and truly thank our partners for their undiluted support in our endeavours.

Every assignment has been an invaluable learning, every association has been truly cherished & every moment has been promising.

This book is dedicated to the numerous talents ("behind the scenes") of this business whose contribution is invaluable & goes unnoticed at every successful event.

Enterprise is a wonderful mix of pursuits, passion and perseverance.
The more one enjoys pushing the limits,
brighter the horizon of abundance.

– Deepak Swaminathan

ABOUT THE AUTHOR

You can connect with the author:-

E-Mail: deepakswaminathan@gmail.com

Twitter: @Deepakswami2571

LinkedIn: Dr Deepak Swaminathan

Facebook: Deepak Swaminathan

Instagram: deepakswaminathan2571